FEMININE FACES

FEMININE FACES

CLOVIS G. CHAPPELL

BAKER BOOK HOUSE
Grand Rapids, Michigan

Copyright 1942 by Whitmore & Stone
Copyright renewal 1970 by Clovis Chappell
Reprinted by Baker Book House
with the permission of
Abingdon Press

ISBN: 0-8010-2355-6

First printing, April 1974
Second printing, November 1978

PHOTOLITHOPRINTED BY CUSHING - MALLOY, INC.
ANN ARBOR, MICHIGAN, UNITED STATES OF AMERICA
1978

CONTENTS

I

THE FROZEN FACE

*"But his wife looked back from behind him,
and she became a pillar of salt."*

GENESIS 19:26

HERE IS A STRIKING STORY THAT IS VERY MODERN
and up to date. But we of today often miss it because of the queer costume in which it is dressed. Here
is a woman warned to flee from a doomed city. She is
further warned that she is not once to look back. She
must keep her face toward the heights. At last she gives
her consent and begins the journey. But she disregards
this latter warning. She has lived in Sodom for a score
of years. Naturally it has some delightful associations.
It has some haunting memories. She cannot break with
it all at once. Therefore, she takes one lingering backward look. The result is disaster. She becomes a
pillar of salt.

How queer it all sounds! Not only is it queer, but it

9

seems to smack of the absurd. What a travesty on a loving God to think that he would punish in this drastic fashion such an innocent something as a backward look. Certainly this old folk story must have been written by one who knew little of either God or man.

But let us not reach this conclusion too quickly. Here is an arresting fact. Jesus read this old story. He looked at this frozen face with its sightless eyes turned back toward Sodom. He read in it not an absurd slander against the love of God. He read in it rather a solemn warning to the men of his day and to those of ours. As he pauses at our side to gaze at this strange figure, he says to us, solemnly, almost sternly, "Remember Lot's wife."

I

Look at the background of this story. A good many years before, Abraham and Lot had left Ur of the Chaldees to journey into the unknown. Abraham believed that he was making this adventure at the call of God. Lot had caught something of the contagion of his faith and enthusiasm and had joined him. For years nothing came of Abraham's mad dream. That is, there was no heir; no son was born to be the father of many nations. But both Abraham and Lot prospered materially. Their immense prosperity brought on strife, and they decided that it would be wise to separate. In fulfillment of this plan they take their stand, I imagine, on a promontory that gives a lookout on all the surrounding country. Then Abraham with fine generosity gives the younger man first choice.

Lot, with an eye for the main chance, begins to look in every direction. Over to the right is a wild rugged country. Here the grass is not luxurious, but the herdsmen can find sustenance for their flocks if they keep moving. But over in the other direction is a marvelously beautiful country. The story says that it looked like the garden of the Lord. As Lot looks on the landscape as the oriental sunlight kisses the dewdrops on the lips of the grasses into a million jewels, he smiles. The scene makes his palms itch. "If I go that way," he says to himself, "I will get on. I will make a pile of money." But even as he looks his smile changes into a frown. What is the matter? He sees the cities of the plain, Sodom and Gomorrah. To him, they are as cesspools in a flower garden, as horrid blemishes on an otherwise lovely face. Thus the scene repels while it appeals.

As he looks in the other direction, he says to himself, "If I go this way I will not make so much money, but I will have a better chance at the values that last. I will have a better chance at God. My children will have a better chance at God. My wife, who is a bit worldly, will have a better chance at God." Thus he stands, making up his mind. That way a better chance at things, this way a better chance at God. It is a choice we have to make and make every day. Which way did Lot go? Here is the tragic answer. "He pitched his tent in the direction of Sodom." He made a wrong choice, and that wrong choice led him in a wrong direction.

Now as he was going in a wrong direction we are not surprised that he reached a wrong goal. We read in the very next chapter after this incident that Lot dwelt in Sodom. That was not his goal when he set out. He was only going in that direction. But little by little he came closer to Sodom till he moved into the city. Then in the chapter of which our text is a part we read that Lot sat in the gate at Sodom. Not only had he moved into Sodom, but he had become mayor of the city. I can well guess the platform on which he ran. He was going to give the city a business administration. That is what every city wants. That is what few cities get. So for a score of years Lot lived and prospered in Sodom. These years might have been years of moral enrichment to Lot and his family and to Sodom as well had he been true to his faith. But he did not change Sodom; Sodom changed him. That is ever the case. If we do not try to change our world for the better, it will change us for the worse. Sodom became for Lot and his wife more than a point on the map. It became an attitude of Godless worldliness.

Then one day heavy news came their way. They were informed that Sodom was going to be destroyed for its wickedness. Of course, that message was in no sense unique. All that was unique about it was that it came in a dramatic fashion, and was carried out in a spectacular and dramatic way. But that same doom is being pronounced again and again. "The soul that sinneth, it shall die." It is pronounced against every Godless city, and against every Godless nation. This sentence, then, that sounds queer and harsh is the language of the whole Bible. It is the language of human history. Our graveyards are littered with nations that have died of their own sin. Sodom then became what Bunyan would call "The City of Destruction."

But while the city was doomed, Lot and his wife were offered an opportunity to escape. They were given the privilege of beginning life anew in the clean atmosphere of the hills. Life in Sodom had been disappointing to both of them in spite of their love for it. They had never been able to forget the faith that had once been theirs. Once along with Abraham they had builded altars. Once they had looked to the heights. Once they knew how to pray. They had been homesick for this better life many times. They had been pained and disgusted by the wickedness of Sodom many times. We read of Lot that they vexed his righteous soul from day to day. And now at last there was a chance for them to escape it all and begin life anew. But they looked at their opportunity with cold and critical eyes. They felt as if God were trying to cheat them out of something. "You must begin life anew," said God's messenger. But their faces did not light up. "Do we have to?" they asked gloomily. "You must be born anew," said Jesus centuries later. And we look at him with reluctant faces and say, "Must we?" forgetting that this "must" is not one of compulsion, but of highest possible privilege.

Not only did these two regard the privilege of beginning anew without enthusiasm; they resolved to postpone acting upon it as long as possible. "Of course," they said, "we must leave Sodom with its moral decay, with its rapidly approaching doom, sometime. Sometime we must go toward the heights. But let us postpone it as long as possible."

Do not be impatient with them. Do not sneer at them. We have acted with the same blindness a thousand times, and with far more light than they had. How many there are who expect to be Christian someday, but desire to put off the hard ordeal as long as possible. They virtually say, "Let me live for myself; let me live apart from God; let me cheat myself of life abundant as long as possible. Let me rob myself of my highest usefulness as long as possible. I want to be a Christian someday, but my motive is not that I might be and do my best. It is only that I might escape the doom of Sodom."

Having postponed their decision till they felt that death was close upon their tracks, Lot and his wife at last turned their backs upon Sodom and made a reluctant start for the hills. But there was no eagerness in their going, no high enthusiasm. This was true of Lot, but it was even more true of Mrs. Lot. The story says, "She looked back from behind him." That is sig-

nificant. Feeling the strong tug of Sodom upon her
soul, seeing no compelling beauty in the heights, she did
not make much progress. She traveled with slow and
reluctant feet. Soon even tortoise-like Lot had out-
stripped her. She found herself cut off from the group.
She said, "I will just take one last look in spite of the
fact that such a look is forbidden." So she turned, and
the volcanic ashes embalmed her. And there she stood
a grotesque statue with her face turned back toward death.

II

What is the meaning of this weird story? Why this
tragic doom? Believe me, there was nothing arbitrary
about it on God's part. Sometimes we read this story
in such a wooden fashion that we fancy that the author
is trying to tell us that God struck this woman dead for
doing so innocent a thing as looking back to the city
where she had lived for a score of years. But this is
not the case at all. This woman was not so much
punished for her sin as she was punished by her sin.
This backward look on her part worked tragedy, I
know. It has worked the same tragedy in countless
millions of lives. It will work the same tragedy in
your life and mine if we give way to it. God is therefore not punishing this woman because he is vindictive
and angry.

Nor are we to think of this act of disobedience on the
part of Mrs. Lot as one born of sheer stubbornness.

She did not reach a certain spot where she planted her feet with grim determination and said, "Beyond this I will never take another step. I have made up my mind that I will neither live in Sodom nor in the heights. From now on I am going to abide exactly where I am." That was not her intention at all. She was going to stop for only a moment. Hers was a temporary pause, as she herself thought. She was a temporary transgressor, even as you and I. No one of us intends to hold on to our sin forever. We are only going to enjoy sin for a season. But that temporary stop became for her, as it may for us, eternal.

What, then, was wrong? It was not the backward look. The backward look was not the disease from which this woman was suffering; it was only a symptom. I knew a young chap some time ago who began to take on extra weight. Getting a bit heavier is no calamity, especially to one who is naturally thin. But it was tragic in the case of this young man. His physician said that his extra weight was a symptom of a deadly disease. This backward look is like the idle word against which Jesus warns. I remember how harsh it seemed to me as a boy that we were to have to give account to God for every idle word. But the idle word is the unguarded word. It is the word that focuses the light upon our souls. It is not the idle word, therefore, that is significant, but the character that the word reveals. Even so this backward look was an indication

16

of a fatal disease of the inner life. It indicated that this woman was suffering from a divided heart.

Here, then, is a word that comes close to every one of us. A divided mind spells tragedy. This is affirmed by the whole Bible. It is most emphatically affirmed by Jesus. There is nothing upon which our Lord insists with greater urgency than the necessity of wholeheartedness. To fail to make up one's mind, to be divided in allegiance is to make discipleship an impossibility. "No man can serve two masters: for either he will hate the one, and love the other; or else he will hold to the one, and despise the other. Ye cannot serve God and mammon." For instance, a young man once came to Jesus all enthusiasm, saying, "Lord, I will follow thee whithersoever thou goest." Do not think for a moment that the heart of Jesus did not warm to that declaration. But as the Master looked at him and read his very soul, he saw that while discipleship made a tremendous appeal, things made a yet greater appeal. Therefore, he gave him this answer: "Foxes have holes, and the birds of the air have nests, but the Son of man hath not where to lay his head." What does Jesus mean? This is not the language of self-pity. The Master is not appealing for sympathy because he is more homeless than the foxes and more destitute than the birds of the air. He is rather emphasizing his own freedom. "I am as free," he declares joyfully, "as these creatures of the wide open spaces. I am not enslaved by things. If you are going to be my disciple, you must be willing to share

17

my independence. You cannot serve God and things."

"Follow me," said Jesus to another friend. That friend had also felt the spell of the Master and was eager to obey. There was but one hindrance. That was his devotion to his father. Therefore this man replied, "Let me first go and bury my father." By this he is not meaning to say that his father is dead. He means this, rather: "My father would be very disappointed and very lonely were I to leave him now to become your disciple. But if you will wait till he is dead, then I will come gladly." But Jesus could not accept any such divided allegiance. Therefore he said, "Let the dead bury the dead; but go thou and preach the kingdom of God."

Then there was a third man who heard the appeal of Jesus and felt his compelling spell. He, too, was perfectly willing to become a disciple, provided he could make his own terms. He was willing to give Jesus any place in his life except first place. Therefore he said, "Let me first go bid them farewell which are at home at my house." "Let me first say good-bye to my people at home," Moffatt translates it. This man had a family. Perhaps he had guests that he felt he could not leave without telling them good-bye. But Jesus answers with solemn earnestness, "No man, having put his hand to the plow, and looking back, is fit for the kingdom." There was no anger in this. It was just a plain statement of fact. A divided mind unfits us for the business of living in every department of life. It makes vital Christianity utterly impossible.

III

But wherein is the divided man an unfit man? What are some of the penalties we pay for being of a divided mind?

1. We miss the joy that is the privilege of the decided. Our most wretched hours are generally hours of indecision. To be unable to decide between two prizes is to experience the pain of missing both. Where did Lot's wife die? She died neither in Sodom nor in the heights. Trying to make the best of both worlds she lost both. I remember a cow we used to have that was fond of jumping fences. She was an awkward creature. She seldom made a really successful jump. Usually she fell upon the fence and hung there. Thus, with her hind feet in one pasture and her fore feet in the other, she would lie and moan, getting nothing out of either pasture. To find real joy in living one must be wholehearted.

2. A divided heart makes us unfit because it robs us of our strength. The strongest of men will accomplish little if he cannot say, "This one thing I do." But an ordinary man can do the impossible if he is a man of one purpose. Listen to this old story again: "His wife looked back from behind." Why had she fallen behind? It was not lack of strength, but a divided will. Never

19

can we travel very swiftly toward the heights if our hearts are in Sodom. If our eyes are looking back to the world, we are not likely to make much progress toward the things of the spirit. A divided heart makes us unfit because it robs us of our joy and of our power to go forward.

3. Finally, indecision ends in disaster. By this I do not mean that disaster always comes in the dramatic fashion in which it came to Lot's wife. We miss the whole point of the story if we think that the tragedy of this woman was her physical death. Her tragedy was not physical, but spiritual. This crude figure with its face turned toward Sodom gives us a photograph of the woman's soul. Sudden death did not turn her face in the wrong direction. The woman herself did the turning. All death did was to freeze that backward looking face so that all the future centuries might see it. Her backward look would have been just as tragic, perhaps even more so, had she lived a hundred years longer.

We read the same lesson in the story of the rich farmer of whom Jesus told. One day while he was congratulating himself on his abundant crops and his well-filled barns, God broke in upon his soliloquy with this harsh word: "Thou fool! this night thy soul shall be required of thee." But why was this man a fool? He was not a fool because death dashed upon him without warning. Had he kept facing in the same direction he would still be a fool, though he had lived for these nineteen centuries. That which made him a fool was the fact that he ignored God. He was an imbecile before death ever came upon the scene. Therefore, all that death did for him was to freeze that imbecile look upon his face that all might see.

This same truth is enforced by this story: When Pompeii was being excavated there was found a body that had been embalmed by the ashes of Vesuvius. It was that of a woman. Her feet were turned toward the city gate, but her face was turned backward toward something that lay just beyond her outstretched hands. The prize for which those frozen fingers were reaching was a bag of pearls. Maybe she herself had dropped them as she was fleeing for her life. Maybe she had found them where they had been dropped by another. But, be that as it may, though death was hard at her heels, and life was beckoning to her beyond the city gates, she could not shake off their spell. She had turned to pick them up, with death as her reward. But it was not the eruption of Vesuvius that made her love pearls more than life. It only froze her in this attitude of greed.

Let us, then, listen once more to these solemn words of our Lord: "Remember Lot's wife." Remember that a wrong choice led to a wrong character. Remember that God gave her a chance to make a new start. Remember that though she took that chance, she took it half-heartedly. Remember that hers was the tragedy of a divided mind. For almost to do a thing is not to do it at all. Almost to be a disciple is to miss knowing Jesus.

Almost to be saved is to be lost. Almost to live is to die. Almost to journey to the heights is to share the fate of Sodom just as really as if we never set a foot outside her gates. "How long go ye limping between the two sides? if Jehovah be God, follow him."

II

THE DESPERATE FACE

*"And she sat over against him, and lifted up
her voice, and wept."*

GENESIS 21:16

I

HERE IS A TRAGIC PICTURE. THE SCENE IS A DESERT. There may be something fascinating about a desert when looked at from a place of safety. I confess that I can gladly gaze upon it by the hour from the window of an air-conditioned car. But that fascination becomes stark horror when one sees this same desert through bloodshot eyes as it tortures with thirst and threatens to become an untimely grave. Such is the case in the story of which our text is a part. As far as the eye can see the weird waste stretches in monotonous ugliness. The hot winds are blowing the sand into ridges that look like the skeleton ribs of some gigantic monster. Over all the parched landscape the heat specters dance. Not a shred of verdant beauty is visible

23

Here and there are a few dry and scraggy bushes whose drab ugliness speak of death far more than of life. In fact everything seems either dying or dead.

Overhead the scene is as depressing as the desert itself. In all that hot and copper sky there is no shred of cloud. Nothing is visible except a cruel and bloody sun that is wounding everything that is not yet wholly dead with arrows of fire. How utterly lifeless is this world of sand and sky! Then in those empty heavens a speck appears, small and black and far away. Then there is another and yet another. These specks are coming nearer. There at least is life. But it is a kind of life that adds to, rather than lessens, the horror of the scene. For these growing specks are vultures, ghastly creatures that have discovered by some queer magic that a table is soon to be spread for them in this hell-like oven. But now everywhere silence reigns, a silence as deep and depressing as that of a funeral vault at midnight.

Suddenly that silence is broken. There is a low moan followed by a feeble cry for water. That cry has come from the tortured lips of a boy who is stretched upon his back under the meager shade of a dwarfed shrub. He is well grown and handsome. At least he was before the sun had burned his face to a crisp, and had cracked his lips, and had caused his tongue to protrude from his mouth on account of thirst. The low cry of this dying boy is followed by another sound that is far louder. That is the abandoned sobbing of a woman. It comes from the lips of Hagar, the mother of the boy. She is siting in the open blaze of the sun, a bowshot away. At her feet is a goatskin water bottle. But that bottle is as dry and parched as the desert itself. Her back is turned to her son and she sobs with a bitterness that is born at once of genuine grief and of burning hate.

II

This tragic scene demands an explanation. How did these two come to be where they are?

The story has an interesting and pathetic background. Years ago a man by the name of Abraham had gone for a brief sojourn into Egypt. This man, though a friend of God, had not lived up to his best during this adventure. It is well that God does not require perfection of his friends or none of us could stand. But when this great man left Egypt to return to Canaan, he took something with him, I imagine, besides a sense of humiliation and failure. That something was a swarthy and intelligent little slave girl by the name of Hagar. Through this transaction about which she was not consulted Hagar found herself in a new world. This was the case physically. She went out of her native Egypt into Canaan. It was even more true in matters of religion. She had not been long in the tent of Abraham till she learned that he possessed a peculiar faith.

His faith was unique in that he worshiped one God. With the gods of Egypt, Isis and Osiris and the rest, he would have nothing to do. No more did he worship the gods of the surrounding tribes. He claimed that such worship was futile since it was his God who had created the heavens and the earth and all that is in them. It was at the call of this God that he had left his boyhood home to journey into the unknown. It was to this God that he looked for daily guidance. But his supreme hope, the one big enthusiasm of his life, was a peculiar promise that God had made him. That was the promise of a son. That son was to be a man of destiny. Through him God was going to give the world a new chance. Through him all the nations of the earth were to be blessed.

Hagar soon learned that Abraham and his wife could talk about little else than this high hope. It was of the very warp and woof of their daily lives. It kept them steady when the skies were gray and the way lonely. In fact they believed so firmly and looked so eagerly for this coming heir that Hagar herself began to share their expectations. Yet, the days wore into weeks, the weeks into months, the months into years, and nothing happened. Meantime Abraham and Sarah had passed out of spring into summer and out of summer into autumn. We are not surprised, therefore, when we see their faith beginning to burn low. By and by, for Sarah at least, it spluttered and went out like a lamp whose oil has failed. "We have either misunderstood God," she said, "or he has let us down. If we do not take matters in hand ourselves, we are going to die in these lonely wilds without an heir. Then it will be as if we had never lived. There is no way out but for you to marry my maid, Hagar."

Abraham, according to the easy morals of that day, fell in with Sarah's plans and took this Egyptian woman for his wife. This marriage, I am sure, was very welcome to Hagar, who had just come to the fresh bloom of womanhood. By and by a son was born. Then it was that the joy of this slave woman knew no bounds. She had been honored far beyond her dreams. She remembered now the great promises that God had given to Abraham's son. She herself would have a part in these promises. In her son, and not in Sarah's all the families of the earth shall be blessed. For years she was privileged to know the joy and honor of these high hopes. Then something happened to change her day into black night. God at last fulfilled his promise to Sarah. The sweet angel of suffering came to her tent, and Isaac was born.

This event brought springtime to the hills of Sarah's heart, but it was a killing frost to Hagar. From that very moment she knew that trouble was ahead for herself and her son. After the birth of Isaac she remained for some months in Abraham's tent, but the whole atmosphere had changed. Hagar no longer had a prominent place. It was easy to see that things were headed toward a tragic climax. The high explosives were being gathered that were likely at any moment to be touched off into a domestic tragedy. Then the fatal day came. There was a celebration in honor of Sarah's son. During this celebration, according to the Authorized Version, Ishmael mocked Isaac. According to the better translation of Moffatt Ishmael played with Isaac. Children are about the only real democrats. They know nothing of distinctions between high and low, rich and poor, class and class. But aristocratic Sarah knew. Therefore she simply could not endure to see her son play with the son of a slave. Besides she was naturally very jealous of this younger wife. Therefore she demanded that Abraham cast out this slave woman with her son.

Her demand was a heavy blow for Abraham. He truly loved Ishmael. I have an idea that he loved Hagar too, and that Sarah knew it. But to keep the peace, he gave a reluctant consent. The author indicates that God told Abram to comply with Sarah's demand. Maybe so. But I cannot but believe that were it not for the insistence of this human voice the voice of God might not have been heard. We often rationalize till we get God's backing for what at first blush we knew to be wrong. But right or wrong, one fateful day Abraham set his wife and son adrift in an unfriendly world, armed only with a bit of bread and water and little experience of traveling alone.

We are given no glimpse of the parting scene. I imagine it must have been a bit lurid. Some of Hagar's words, I am sure, could have been safely written only on asbestos. Years ago I had an excellent woman in my church who taught a large class of women. It so happened that this good woman was orthodox to a painful degree. One day she had a meeting at which the husbands of the members of her class were guests. Among those on the program was a young woman who was a reader of rare ability. This strict teacher asked her in advance what she was going to read. "A Bible story," came the highly satisfactory answer. And so she did. She read an imaginary dialogue between Hagar and Abraham as they separated. It was well written and equally well read. Really it was terrific. In fact, it was so bitter that had I met Abraham on my way home, I fear I should have ducked down the alley and have refused to speak to him.

How much truth there may have been in this imaginary scene it is not ours to say. I have an idea there was quite a bit. No woman could rise to the heights to which Hagar had risen, then drop to the position of an outcast without bitterness. Then there was the biting injustice of it all. She knew that she was far more sinned against than sinning. She knew further that, whatever her own fault, Ishmael was blameless. But here she was packed off with nothing but a bit of bread and water. Blinded by tears of grief and anger, she naturally soon became hopelessly lost. For long hours she traveled in circles, not knowing one point of the compass from another. At last, with water exhausted, spent in body, bereft of hope, she had flung her son under the shade of a shrub. Then, without the courage to see him die, she had gone a bowshot away, and had sat down to sob over her wrongs and over the loss of all she held dear. Thus we find her, a picture of utter desperation.

III

But to this hopeless woman relief came. It was relief not for her alone, but for her son as well. How did it come about?

1. God asked this desperate woman a question. The first move toward our salvation is always made, not by ourselves, but by our Lord. Here is the question: "What aileth thee, Hagar?" As we would put it today, "Hagar, what is the matter with you?" On the surface it seems like a rather shallow and annoying question. I can imagine Hagar could have given a volcanic answer to that question. "Do you ask what is the matter with me after what I have suffered? Do you ask what is ailing me when I am at the end of everything, when every hope, every dream, every love has fallen dead before my eyes?" But I think this question did two things for Hagar.

First, it told her something about God. When God said, "What is the matter with you, Hagar?" he was trying to tell this woman that he knew her desperate plight. "I know that there is something the matter. I know how you are suffering. I know how your heart is breaking. You have gone out into the wilderness and lost your way. Losing yourself, you have also lost your son. Even now you do not know where you are.

But though you have lost yourself, I have not lost you. I know all about you." No more has God lost you. It may be that your friends have lost you. It may be that your loved ones have lost you. Your last letter from home was returned because of a wrong address. But God knows all about you.

Not only was there the realization of God's knowledge in this question, but also of his interest. "What aileth thee, Hagar?" God was asking that as a mother might ask it of her sobbing child. "I know there is something wrong. Remember that your pain is my pain, your grief is my grief. Tell me about it. I will listen to it because I care. It will help you to unpack your heart with words." There is often relief in confession, even if our confession is to one weak as ourselves. But how much more is this the case when we confess to God. In his presence we can make bare our very hearts. To him we can tell those tragic stories that we could not tell to any other. God is inviting Hagar to do as another woman did in the presence of Jesus centuries later. "She fell down before him and told him all the truth."

Not only was this question a revelation of God's knowledge of Hagar and of his interest in her, but also of his power to help. "What aileth thee, Hagar?" God is asking. By which he is saying, "Whatever it is, bring it to me and I will help you. You have given up, but I have not. You are hopeless, but I am the God of hope. You are at the end of your strength, but I am

31

not at the end of mine. However tragic your situation may be, though there is nothing else that you can do, there is always something else that I can do. Remember that man's extremity may always be God's opportunity. I know, I am interested, I am able. Therefore tell me your story. Put your case in my hands." Thus this question spoke to Hagar of God.

Not only did this question tell Hagar something about God; it also told her something about herself. "What is the matter with you, Hagar? Look at yourself. Look how quick you are to give up. See what a mess you are making of your own life as well as that of your boy. I know that Sarah has wronged you. I know that Abraham has let you down. But that does not give you the right to destroy yourself and your son by yielding to despair and hate." Surely that is a sane word. However much you and I may have suffered, however great the injustice done us, there can be no excuse for our throwing down our own responsibilities. Nothing can give us the right to give over the fight and sit down and wreck ourselves and others by our cowardice and self-pity. Thus God began this recovery by asking a question that flashed a bit of light into his own face and also into the face of Hagar.

2. His next step in this recovery was a word of assurance. "Fear not; for God hath heard the voice of the lad where he is." That is an arresting word. Hagar does not hear the voice of the lad any more. She has turned her back on him and left him to die alone.

She excuses herself for this by telling herself that she cannot bear to see him suffer. She cannot stand by and witness his pain. But God says, "I am standing by. Your agony in comparison to mine is as a glowworm to a sunrise. Yet, I am standing by. In all his affliction I am afflicted. Not only so, but I have heard his word-less prayer. I have heard and am going to help."

How amazing is this interest on the part of God in one who was only a boy, and the son of a slave at that! This Bible is an old book, yet its attitude toward child-hood is wonderfully modern and up to date. Children have little place in other ancient books. Among the ancients, childhood was just a troublesome period that had to be endured en route to something worth while. It was to be tolerated only as a preliminary to manhood and womanhood. But the Bible, even the Old Testament, sets the child in the midst. In spite of the fact that it was written so long ago it fairly laughs and sings and shouts with children. Here is God listening to the cries of a dying lad. His is the same attitude that centuries later characterized the Christ who gathered little children in his arms to bless them. "Fear not; I have heard the voice of the lad where he is."

3. The third step in recovery was a positive command. "Arise, lift up the lad, and hold him in thy hand." That is a revealing word. This mother had let go her boy. She had given him up for lost. In fact, God tells us, she was wrong. We are always wrong when we act in that fashion. No wrong done to our-

selves, no ghastly wickedness on the part of our children can give us the right to turn from them and to give them up for lost. However hopeless the situation may seem, however worthless and wayward our sons may have become, God's call is still this, "Hold him in thy hand." Yes, and in thy heart as well. It is the mothers and fathers who never give up that win. "Arise, lift up the lad, and hold him in thy hand." And Hagar had the courage to obey.

4. When she obeyed, God helped her to take the next step toward recovery. "And God opened her eyes, and she saw a well of water." How amazing! What are we to understand by this? Is the author trying to tell us that God by his miraculous power suddenly dug a well for Hagar in the desert? By no means. The well had been there all the time. All through those hours of agony it had been offering its life-giving water. But Hagar was so taken up with her own wrongs, she was so blinded by her own bitterness that she could not see it. Even those two disciples going home after the crucifixion failed at first to recognize the risen Christ. Their eyes were so fixed on a tragic yesterday that they could not see a radiant today. Hagar's gaze was so fixed on herself that she missed seeing the spring. But when she obeyed, she discovered.

This is ever the case. For this well in the desert is a symbol of our Lord himself. It is a symbol of him who said, "Every one that drinketh of this water shall thirst again: but whosoever drinketh of the water that I shall give him shall never thirst." Our Lord is always offering us himself, but some of us, as Hagar, are so busy looking at our difficulties and discouragements that we do not see him. Sorely wounded, we have grown peevish and quit trying. "Arise," says God, "lift up the friend, the loved one for whom you have lost hope. Lift up the old dreams, the old convictions, the old ideals. Pick up the task that you have thrown down. Set your feet once more on the road that you have abandoned. Then you too will see the Fountain." This is true because when we are willing to obey we come to know; when we are willing to give life we come truly to live.

5. The final step in this recovery is very tender and very beautiful. When Hagar at last had seen the well, she did not hurry her son off, saying, "Yonder is a well; go and drink." No; this is the story: "She went, and filled the bottle with water, and gave the lad drink." How true to life that is! This lad was so parched, so benumbed and stupefied, that he needed somebody to bring the water to him. He got his chance at the hands of his mother. How many of us got our first glimpse of God by looking into eyes that were homes of silent prayer. For in Christ the believer finds more than satisfaction for himself; he finds it for others as well. That is what Jesus meant by this thrilling word, "If any man thirst, let him come unto me and drink. He that believeth on me, as the Scripture hath said, out of his inner life shall flow rivers of living water."

III

THE SCHEMING FACE

"Upon me be thy curse, my son."

GENESIS 27:13

ONE OF THE BEAUTIFUL MIRACLES POSSIBLE IN OUR world is that an ugly duckling may change into a swan. But it is equally possible that the most beautiful of swans may become an ugly duckling. We have it in our power to be born anew, to be born from above. We also have it in our power to be born from beneath. This latter is what seems to have happened to charming and vivacious Rebekah. Her morning is possessed with a brightness that almost dazzles us. But the brightness and beauty do not last. Soon the shadows begin to gather. By and by the night steals down, black and dreary and without a star. Rebekah's eventide is black enough. But it seems all the more tragic because she

36

made such a beautiful beginning, she had such a bright morning.

I

Look at the brightness of the morning. Her story begins in an atmosphere that is redolent of romance and poetry.

As the scene opens we see two old men in earnest conversation. These two men bear the relationship of employer and employee. Not only so, but they are friends. Then there is also the bond of a common faith in God. One of them, Abraham by name, is one of the outstanding characters of the Old Testament. He is a man so vitally religious that he is known as the Friend of God. He represents religion at its best. Even the writers of the New Testament, when they seek to show us what sainthood is at its beautiful best, have a way of pointing back to this man who one day left Ur of the Chaldees, at the call of God, to journey into the unknown. They show us that in spite of the fact all his great hopes seem to be coming to nothing he still holds on, firmly leaning his back against the promises of God. He is saying boldly, "I know that God did speak to me, and I know that at the last long last what God says must come to pass."

But while Abraham is quite sure that God will keep his promise he is equally sure that he can do so only through his own co-operation. He has journeyed into this unknown land that God through him might make a new beginning. But he knows that this new beginning is likely to be impossible if his son, Isaac, marries one of the pagan women of Canaan. Therefore he is here exacting a promise from his faithful steward that he will not choose a pagan wife for his young master. He is pledging him to go to distant Haran that he may find a girl who will share his faith in God. Even in that distant day Abraham realized how hard it is for a man to stand loyal to his faith when he does not have the backing of his wife.

In the next scene this faithful steward, in compliance with his promise, has made the long journey to Haran. He reaches the city at eventide. The girls are coming out with their water pitchers upon their shoulders to draw water from the well. This loyal steward, sharing the faith of his master, then prays a very simple prayer. He asks God to give him good speed. He asks further that God give to him insight into the character of the girl that he is to choose for his master. "Grant," he seems to say, "that she may be generous and kind. In proof of this may the one who willingly serves me be the girl of thy choice."

No sooner had he finished his prayer when he opens his eyes to get his first sight of Rebekah. He looks upon her with vast approval. She is vigorous, vivacious, and beautiful. Then he hurries forward with his request. "Will you give me a drink, please?" Her answer to this question is to be the test of her fitness. Will she be kind to a travel-stained old man who has no appeal except his need? That is a fine test in any day. Rebekah measures up. At once she responds by lowering her water pitcher and giving the old man a drink. Then she looks at the camels, ten in all. It will take a lot of water to supply them. But with eager enthusiasm she offers her help, saying, "I will give thy camels to drink also." Thus this old man is convinced that she is not only beautiful outwardly, but beautiful within, beautifully generous and beautifully kind.

Upon making this discovery he asks of her family, then presents her with some choice jewelry, golden bracelets and golden earrings. They must have been of unusual value. Having received them, Rebekah hurries back to her home to break the amazing news and to display her wonderful treasures. Those jewels at once catch the eye of at least one member of her family, her brother Laban. Upon seeing this evidence of wealth he indicates a trait of character that becomes more and more conspicuous with the passing of the years. He has an eye for gain. Therefore he rushes out to the old steward with eager welcome upon his lips. "Come in, thou blessed of the Lord," he urges with enthusiasm.

This invitation the steward eagerly accepts. Having been received within the bosom of the family he at once tells his errand. "Abraham," he declares, "under the blessings of God has become a great man. He has come to possess vast wealth. The heir to this great estate is the child of his old age, Isaac. It is in quest of a wife for this rich young chieftain that I am come. I have chosen Rebekah, if she is willing to go." When the family hears this they wisely decided to leave the decision to the one most vitally concerned. Therefore they call this charming young girl and put to her this big question: "Wilt thou go with this man?" Promptly she answers, "I will go." Thus we see that Rebekah is not only a kind and generous young woman, but also a woman of decision and of courage.

Just what motives actuate her in making this decision it is impossible to say. Perhaps she herself could not fully have given the real reasons for her choice. Her motives are doubtless mixed, as ours so often are. I love to believe that her decision is due in part to her faith. She has heard that God is going to bless all the nations of the earth through the family of Abraham. Perchance she makes her choice because of an eager desire to help. Along with this there are surely some less lofty motives. I think one of them is the love of adventure and romance. The long journey, the meeting and the marrying of a man whose face she has not seen appeal to the daring and romantic in her. Then, I am sure that she is none the less eager to go because she knows that her future husband is one of the richest men in the land.

But, be the causes what they may, she breaks with all the old and familiar to take her journey into the unknown. As she makes this long journey there are doubtless times when she is happy and there are other times when she is a bit sad and half afraid. But the wise old steward seeks to beguile the toilsome hours by telling her of the greatness of Abraham and of the goodness of the man that she is going to marry. At last she sees somebody walking in the fields. A quicker beating of her own heart leads her to guess who it is. When she learns that it is her future husband, she dismounts from her camel, the two meet, and immediately they are married. Of course they are strangers to each other, as many are who marry today. But in spite of this their marriage should have been highly successful. They should have lived happily ever after. But such was not the case. The morning that had dawned so brightly soon came to be darkened by shadows.

II

Look at the gathering shadows. How do we account for them? Isaac and Rebekah seem to have begun at once to grow apart instead of growing together. Husbands and wives always grow in one direction or the other. Let me urge upon all young couples the necessity of growing together instead of growing apart. Remember that you will love each other far better twenty years from now or far less. Isaac and Rebekah were naturally not deeply in love when they married. But they loved each other even less as the years went by. At last their marriage rotted down and fell apart. They never divorced each other in the courts of the land, but they became divorced in their hearts.

Whose was the fault? We can give the usual answer. It was the fault of both. Isaac was a good man, but his goodness was of the passive type. Then he was gripped by a mother-complex. We read this significant sentence in connection with their marriage, "Isaac was comforted after his mother's death." That means that Rebekah not only had to be a wife to her husband, but a mother as well. Little by little she had to take over the management of affairs. By thus assuming larger responsibilities she became stronger, while Isaac became weaker. Then there followed another evil result; Isaac, knowing himself managed and henpecked, little by little lost his self-respect. He came more and more to live within himself, and to think only of his own personal comfort. Naturally Rebekah came little by little to lose respect for her childish husband, and to look upon him with contempt.

Of course we read some of this between the lines. But we can be sure of the truth of it because we ourselves have witnessed just such happenings. I do not think it is being unduly critical of wives to say that many of them, even the best, will henpeck their husbands if they can. But having achieved their goal, they are never proud of the results. For there is this fundamental difference between men and women. Every husband in order to be happy and contented must feel that his wife looks up to him in some fashion. It is equally true that no wife can be genuinely happy who cannot for some reason look up to her husband. Since this is true, if a wife is wise she contrives to look up, even if she has to put her husband on a stepladder or herself get into a cellar in order to do it. Isaac and Rebekah did not get on well because, while the one was too soft, the other was too hard and aggressive.

But after some score of years there came an event that should have brought these two closer together. After long waiting Rebekah at last became a mother. She gave birth to twins, Esau and Jacob. Both these boys were her very own. Both were the sons of Isaac. These two had shared with God in their creation. Naturally these two boys ought to have gripped the hearts of both parents and to have drawn them closer together. But such was not the case. Instead of bringing them closer together they pushed them further apart. This was the case because each parent picked a favorite. How silly and how wicked! Yet I know a couple who are doing the same thing. In that home are two children, a boy and a girl. The father claims the son, while the daughter belongs to the mother.

Isaac gave his love to Esau. It is easy to understand this. Esau was a vigorous and magnificent animal. The writer to the Hebrews says that he was a sensualist. That means, not that he was a corrupt man, but that he lived for the satisfaction of his senses. For instance, one day he sold his birthright for a mess of beans. He was interested only in the seen. He did not hate God, he simply ignored him. He was interested in the chase and in a good dinner. He had no thought for tomorrow. He was totally without ambition. Easy-going

Isaac felt comfortable in the presence of this sensual son. He also liked the good dinners that he prepared. "Isaac loved Esau, because he did eat of his venison." What a pitiful commentary on the character of this good man who had grown prematurely old, and had degenerated into a mere "blind mouth."

But aggressive and ambitious Rebekah had a contempt for Esau as she did for Isaac. Jacob was a boy after her heart. He was shrewd and needed a lot of watching. His conception of God was mean and unworthy. But in spite of this Jacob did have an appreciation of religion. He also had a sense of the worth of tomorrow. Then, too, he was ambitious to be somebody and to do something in the world. Rebekah therefore loved him because he was so like herself. In fact she loved him so well that she was willing to do almost anything to further his prospects. Rebekah was fundamentally a schemer, and a dishonest schemer at that. She believed that a crooked line was the shortest distance between two points. She was not a good sport. She had no conception of playing the game according to the rules. In fact she was so cheap as to become an evesdropper. She was good at listening at keyholes and at using the information so gained for her own ends.

One day this patient listener was rewarded. She heard her prematurely old and blind husband talking to Esau. He told his favorite that the end of the journey was near. Therefore he urged Esau to go into the forest and kill a deer and prepare him a good dinner. Having eaten he would give him his blessing. Isaac could not think of blessing anybody on an empty stomach. As soon as Esau received this commission he went out to do as his father had commanded. Though he was a sensualist and without ambition he still desired at least the material rewards that he thought would come from his father's blessings.

But Rebekah made up her mind to steal this blessing for her favorite. So she called Jacob and told him what she had heard. She ordered him to kill two kids and let her prepare a good meal for Isaac. Thus they would beat Esau to the draw. Jacob himself threatened to balk at this glaring bit of crookedness. This was the case not because he was honest, but because he was afraid that he might be caught. Rebekah and Jacob were alike in this; the one sin, to their way of thinking, was the sin of getting caught. "My father," said Jacob, "might detect the fraud and give me a curse rather than a blessing." "Upon me be thy curse," came the firm answer of this scheming woman. Thus they went through with the deception with complete success. Thus Jacob was able to steal the blessing that rightfully belonged to Esau.

III

Then came the final night.

What had Rebekah said when Jacob was about to falter? This: "Upon me be thy curse." By this she was saying, "I will take all the blame. Whatever evil comes of this dirty deception shall be mine." In so saying she was speaking even more truly than she realized. As a result of her scheming a curse did come upon her. She, as all others, reaped as she sowed. Part of that curse was inward and invisible.

She paid the penalty that all pay who try to build upon a lie. She may have at last been driven back to God through loneliness and heartache. If not, she lost herself. Then she lost her family. She and Isaac had been far enough apart before, but after this treachery they must have glared at each other across yet wider chasms. She was cursed in the complete loss of Esau. Easy-going animal that he was, he could not but hate the mother who had dealt with him with such utter injustice. She was cursed further by the knowledge that she had driven a wedge between her two sons. Esau not only hated his mother but his brother as well. So intense was this hatred that it became necessary for Jacob to flee for his life. Thus she lost her favorite. One day she had to tell Jacob that his brother was bent on vengeance. Then, realizing that she was losing him, yet trying to soften the blow, she said, "Go away for a few days till Esau forgets." But those few days lengthened into weeks, the weeks into months, the months into twenty long years. At last Rebekah died without ever seeing her son again. Thus by her dishonest scheming she did bring a curse upon herself.

But what is more tragic still, the curse that she

brought did not stop with herself. Such a curse never does. Nobody ever inherits a blessing alone. If I enter into fellowship with God, that very fact gives me something to share with others. But if I fail and fall, I do not fall alone. Isaac bore part of Rebekah's curse, Esau bore part of it. In his bitterness he threw himself away on pagan wives. He thus became the father of a nation that became a thorn in the side of Israel for centuries to come.

But perhaps the blackest curse was the one that Rebekah put upon her favorite son Jacob. She sent him into the world with a twisted mind. She sent him out believing that he could build solidly and permanently upon a lie. She sent him out convinced that in a world where the law of sowing and reaping works with mathematical exactness he could have cunning to reverse this law. He could gather grapes of thorns and figs of thistles. She cursed her son with the damning conviction that sin could be made to pay. I am glad to know that through the good grace of God Jacob was brought to repentance. But this was not because of his mother's influence; it was in spite of it.

Here then is a woman who had a great opportunity. She made a fine beginning, but she messed up her life. She also brought suffering to those nearest to her. Countless thousands whose faces she never saw suffered through her sin. Yet she was not a bad woman. She was a woman of many fine qualities. She was even religious. Her fundamental blunder was that she thought of God as one whom she could bend to her purposes—even though they were crooked purposes—instead of a Father who in love longed to lay hold on her and use her for his high and holy purposes. Holding this false faith she was wrong on the inside and in consequence exerted a wrong influence. Thus a life that might have left a track of light across all the years became little more than a curse.

IV

THE BRILLIANT FACE

"For I brought thee up out of the land of Egypt, and redeemed thee out of the house of servants; and I sent before thee Moses, Aaron, and Miriam."

MICAH 6:4

I

"I SENT BEFORE THEE, MOSES, AARON, AND MIRIAM." Here is a woman who stands on a basis of equality with her two gifted brothers. She is far ahead of her time. This is evident from a glance at her story.

1. Miriam is the first woman that we meet on the pages of the Bible who has a career outside the home. In that distant day and for many centuries following there was but one honorable vocation open to woman. That vocation of wifehood and motherhood. She was significant as the wife of some man. She was significant as a mother. She found her one place of power in the home. We are old-fashioned enough to believe that her place of supreme usefulness is still here. We believe that the woman who deliberately turns aside from this

49

high vocation abdicates her supremest throne and stops
her ears to "the deepest and sweetest secret of human
blessedness."

But while we believe that woman comes to her best
in the home as the keeper of the gate of life, we are
glad that this is not her only vocation. The modern
woman enjoys a freedom of which her sister of a few
years ago never dreamed. Today roadways lead di-
rectly from her door into practically every vocation into
which man is entering. As far back as 1920, of the 572
gainful occupations in America, 537 had been successfully entered by woman. There were even then only
thirty-five gainful occupations that were exclusively
masculine. The number would perhaps be even smaller
today. Millions of women are now finding careers outside the home. Nor are we to criticize them for this.
The tasks that they used to do in the home have been
carried outside. Multitudes of women must therefore
go outside the home to work or not work at all. But
at the vanguard of these workers we must place Miriam.

The particular career to which Miriam felt herself
called was that of assisting her brothers in the building
of a new nation. She was in a sense a politician. She
was a stateswoman. How much she added to the success of the enterprise of making Israel into a new nation
we cannot definitely say. It would be perhaps equally
difficult to say how much the modern woman has im-
proved the political situation since she has received the
ballot. It used to be claimed that if woman were only

allowed to vote, age-old abuses such as liquor and war would be made impossible. Of course this has not come to pass. As almost everyone else, I believe in the right of woman to vote and to pursue a political career. This is the case in spite of the fact that I am not sure that these privileges have so far been of any real help either to herself or to others. But they are her right none the less.

2. The second interesting fact about Miriam is that it would seem that she was an old maid. If this is the case she is the first spinster we meet on the pages of the Bible. Just why she failed to marry we are not told. I think it is possible for us to form an intelligent opinion. She perhaps had two good reasons. First, she was so interested in her career that she had little time for matters of the heart. It may be that men did not interest her, that she had no time for the thoughtless creatures. Not being interested in men, they were naturally not greatly interested in her.

Then there was a second reason. Miriam was a very brilliant woman. She was far more intelligent and thoughtful than most men of her time. That in itself put her at a disadvantage. Highly intelligent and cultivated women are often at a disadvantage in the marriage market. It is in the nature of man to desire to be looked up to. He is prone to think well of the woman who makes him think well of himself. But brilliant Miriam made her wooer feel cheap and uncomfortable. He was eager to be looked up to, but this she could not do without getting into a cellar. Had she cared enough to have pretended to be a bit stupid, had she sent her dullard wooer away feeling that he had been brilliant in conversation, he might have come back and they might have lived happily ever afterward. But having sent him away feeling a bit like a toad, the next night he went to the other end of the street to see a girl who might have been characterized as beautiful but dumb. But, be the causes what they may, Miriam, the career woman, did not marry.

3. Not only was Miriam a woman with a vocation outside the home, but according to the record she was divinely called to that vocation. Nobody doubts the call of Moses and Aaron. But this woman who had been rocked in the arms of the same mother is represented as being just as divinely called as her brothers. That is out of the ordinary. The Jews, along with all other ancient peoples, looked upon woman as an inferior. Jesus alone of all the great religious teachers treated men and women as equals. He never spoke any message to men that could not have been spoken to women, or to women that he could not have spoken to men. To him they were all the children of a common Father and of equal standing before God. But this took place many centuries before Jesus came. Therefore it is astonishing to hear this author say that Miriam was as truly called to her career as Moses and Aaron were called to theirs.

II

How did this divinely called woman get on with her task? We get only brief glimpses of her. Save for one ugly blot upon her career she seems to have given a good account of herself.

1. The first glimpse we get of Miriam is on the banks of the Nile. She is a girl of perhaps twelve or fourteen years of age. She is doing what older sisters have done countless millions of times. She is playing nursemaid to a baby brother. This baby is destined to make history on a large scale. But being a part of a slave population that is growing too rapidly he has come into life with a sentence of death pronounced against him. But his pious father and mother cannot bear to give him up. He is such a beautiful baby. The story says that they saw that he was a proper child. Certainly. That is the kind of child yours is. All parents have been blessed by such children. Therefore, these two take a basket and line it with pitch and prayer, put the little fugitive into it, then put the strange vessel to float among the rushes on the waters of the Nile. It was this queer ship with its priceless cargo that Miriam is set to guard.

I can imagine she felt the task monotonous enough at first. Then something happened. Suddenly she heard voices. Looking in the direction from which those voices came she saw a group of women making their way toward the river. She saw with terror that they were headed toward the very spot where the baby was hidden. Then her terror became all the greater when she recognized that the leader of this group of women was none other than the princess herself. If this daughter of Pharaoh should find the child, of course there would be no hope. As Miriam held her breath she saw these women go straight to where the little boat was anchored. Then one of the maids saw it and drew it to shore. There were cries of amazement and pity. Then the princess was stretching out her arms to this beautiful baby.

We have called Miriam brilliant. We need no further proof of her keen intellectuality than the skill and tact with which she handled this situation. Watching the princess with sharp eyes, she was quick to see that Moses had nothing to fear at her hands. She became quite sure that his life was going to be spared. But for Moses merely to live was not enough. He must be trained for that future of which his pious parents were dimly dreaming. That this might be the case she must see to it that his training be put in the right hands. If an Egyptian woman should become his nurse he would grow up an Egyptian. This would never do. This boy must be trained by a Hebrew woman, by his own mother at that.

But how was all this to be arranged? Miriam was keen enough to know that it would never do for her to tell the princess, "I am the baby's sister. I can get his own mother as his nurse." The princess would have been too wise to have accepted an arrangement like that.

She would have known that under those conditions this baby would never really be truly hers. Miriam therefore said nothing about the parentage of the child; she only proposed to get him a nurse. When her offer had been accepted she hurried away, and soon Moses was back in the arms of his own mother. Thus restored, Moses naturally came to share the faith of those that guided his young and tender years. But I doubt if this arrangement, so fruitful in good, would have been made except for the keen intelligence of this poised and courageous girl, Miriam.

2. The next glimpse we get of Miriam is on the shores of the Red Sea. She is now a mature woman. She has become one of the leaders of her people. But it would seem that she is exercising her leadership chiefly among the women. The Israelites have just made a marvelous escape. Yesterday the Red Sea was before them and the forces of Pharoah were pressing hard upon their heels. Today they have crossed that sea and the bodies of the soldiers of Pharaoh's once-proud army are being spit out upon the shore. No wonder such deliverance is an occasion of great joy. The people are singing. But it is Miriam who leads the song. It is a song not in praise of themselves, but in praise of their God who has triumphed gloriously. It is a song of the past. But its purpose is to prepare those delivered people for the difficulties of the future. Wher Paul wrote, "forgetting those things which are behind, and reaching forth unto those things which are before,"

he was not urging us to forget all that is behind. That would be at once impossible and ruinous. We ought never to forget God's amazing mercies and his wonderful deliverances. "Remember that thou wast a bondman in the land of Egypt, and the Lord thy God redeemed thee." This poetic woman was therefore a source of courage and inspiration to her people.

III

But there is one tragic blot upon her career. One day she allowed herself to become bitter and rebellious. Or, to state it more accurately, one day she allowed the bitterness and rebellion that she had long been nursing in her heart to come into the open. One day she dared speak out the rebellious sentiments that had been torturing her for no telling how long. Her fault was not a small one. This is indicated by the fact that she seems to have taken her name from this single event. Her name came to signify bitterness and rebellion.

Here is the story: "And Miriam and Aaron spake against Moses . . . . and they said, Hath the Lord indeed spoken only by Moses? hath he not spoken also by us?" Upon the surface their criticism does not seem such an ugly sin. That this one bit of fretful faultfinding should darken an otherwise useful career seems hardly fair. But even if it is not entirely just, it is what often happens. It is easily possible for one false step to blight an otherwise beautiful career. One single deed of dishonesty on the part of the cashier of a bank can blot out ten thousand deeds that were strictly honest. It is therefore not without reason that we seem prone to judge folks by heir faults rather than by their virtues. If giving Miriam a bad name because of one single rebellious act therefore seems a bit unfair, it is a common blunder, one that we make again and again.

Nor are we necessarily wrong when we do this. The justice of this name becomes evident when we realize that this word of rebellion was a symptom of the disease from which Miriam was suffering rather than the disease itself. Her bitter words came from a bitter heart. The pretext for her criticism of Moses was his wife. Moses had married a woman who was not a Jewess. She brought this matter up, I think, because she knew it would be so easy to create a prejudice against Moses because of it. I am quite sure that she herself keenly resented this sister-in-law. This she did for perhaps two reasons: First, because she was a foreigner. Her patriotism may have been made up as much of hatred for non-Jews as of love for her own people. Then she was far older than Moses. She had helped to raise him. She felt a bit as if Moses were her son. In her criticism, therefore, she was playing the part of the mother-in-law at her worst.

But this complaint against Moses on account of his wife was mainly a pretext. Her chief objection to Moses was that he was more prominent and more powerful than herself. Being greater in character and greater in ability, he was the natural leader of Israel.

This filled brilliant Miriam with envy. She was evidently a very ambitious woman. She was able and knew it. Therefore it filled her with inward rage that she did not have a place of greater prominence. So bitter did she become that she enlisted Aaron in her scheme and sought to discredit the leadership of Moses by claiming that God was accustomed to speak by her and by Aaron quite as genuinely as by her more distinguished brother.

As a result of this bitter outbreak, the story tells us that she was smitten with leprosy. She became the victim of a deadly disease. Leprosy throughout the Bible is a symbol of sin. The inner sickness of the soul came to be written upon her face. We have seen the same thing happen many times. Here is one who is constantly giving way to envy, or to anger that hardens into hate. Those evil passions soon write their names in letters of ugliness upon such a face. Miriam allowed herself to become self-centered and envious. Such evils are deadly. They destroy just as surely and just as inevitably as does such an incurable disease as leprosy. Thus this brilliant woman who might have been at once happy and useful became wretched and hurtful because she let her selfish ambition get the better of her.

Now if you gave attention to the reading of this story you remember that it reads like this: "Miriam and Aaron spake against Moses." But it was Miriam alone who was punished. That sounds a bit unfair. Why did not Aaron share the leprosy with his sister? For the very simple reason, I am sure, that he did not share Miriam's envy and bitterness. He was not a leader in this evil business; he was a more or less passive tool. Aaron had very glaring faults, but they were not of the active and aggressive type. The truth is that he was a bit of a weakling.

Here, for instance, is a story that gives us a clear view of this soft and weak man. Moses has gone away into the mountains. He has been away so long that his childish followers have made up their minds that he is never going to return. Therefore, they come to Aaron with this request: "Up, make us gods, which shall go before us; for as for this Moses . . . . we know not what is become of him." And Aaron, eager to please, complied with their request. He made a golden calf which the people celebrated by a wild party. When Moses returned, he indignantly called Aaron upon the carpet. But the weakling did not have the courage to confess his guilt. According to him the golden calf was nothing but an ugly accident. In fact when the creature came into being nobody was more surprised than Aaron himself. Here is his explanation: "I cast [the gold] into the fire, and there came out this calf." This is the alibi of a weakling.

Miriam had been with Aaron far more than she had been with Moses. Very early Moses had gone away to live at the palace of Pharaoh. From thence he had fled to the Midian desert. But Miriam had grown up with Aaron. She was older and of far tougher fiber. In thus fostering rebellion she was the leader. Here, as doubtless on many other occasions, she molded Aaron to her will. Therefore, while the role of this weak brother was bad enough it was not so bad as that of his stronger sister. It was this inner bitterness that faced her toward inevitable death.

IV

But this story has a brighter side. Though Miriam became a moral leper through her ambitious and envious spirit, she did not die that way. She was cured. There took place in her life that ever-new miracle of forgiveness. Her bitterness was changed to sweetness and her rebellion to meekness. As in the case of Naaman her flesh came back as the flesh of a little child. She found herself once more in a place of honor and usefulness among her people. This does not mean that her sin made no difference. Through her moral failure she herself suffered. But, as always, her sin did not stop with herself. Though she was forgiven and restored the whole enterprise in which she was engaged was slowed down by her rebellion. The story tells us that for one week all progress was stopped. When we fail to be at our best we hurt not only ourselves, but we hurt others. To allow bitterness in our own hearts is to create bitterness in the hearts of others. We only help our fellows to go forward as we ourselves go forward in the fellowship of our Lord. That was the case then, it will be so forever.

But we are not only interested in the fact that Miriam was restored, we are also interested in how her restoration was brought about. She had done Moses a great wrong. She had sought to discredit him, to weaken his influence, and to make his already heavy task far harder. Resentment on the part of Moses, therefore, would have been very easy. It would have been all the easier because the one who was seeking to do him harm was his own sister. He might have expected such conduct from a foe, but certainly not from one who was so near to him, and who claimed to be devoted to the same enterprise to which he was giving his life. There are no hates more bitter than those that sometimes exist within the family circle.

But Moses refused to meet anger with anger or hate with hate. He refused to answer criticism with criticism. He might have given Miriam a piece of his mind. He might have told her that he would never speak to her again. He might thus have caused her to die in bitterness. He might thus have gone to the end of his own journey with his heart full of hate. But instead he took Christ's way. He was a Christian centuries before the miracle of Bethlehem. He freely forgave her. Not only so, but he undergirded her by his prayers. This is the only wise method of dealing with an enemy. Anger may destroy an enemy, but that is purely negative. It is love and love alone that can make our foes to become our friends. Thus

Moses saved both himself and Miriam by this simple method of Jesus: "Bless them that curse you, ... pray for them which despitefully use you, and persecute you." This is the weapon that we are slowest to try. But it is the one weapon by which we can hope to save both ourselves and our world.

V

THE FIGHTING FACE

"Until that I, Deborah, arose."

JUDGES 5:7

HERE IS AN ANCIENT JOAN OF ARC SINGING A FIERCE song of battle. She is rejoicing over the vast difference that her coming has made. She feels that where she has fought victory has given place to defeat, that where she has farmed "the wilderness and the solitary place have become glad, and the desert has rejoiced and blossomed as the rose." Her coming has made a difference. Of course, that is true of all of us. None of us leave the world just as we found it. We either help or hinder, we either lift up or drag down. We are a part of the remedy or we are a part of the disease. We make for life or we make for death.

Just what difference has your presence made? What

has it done for your home, for your church, for your community, for your world? All some of us do is to make life a bit harder. I read again the other day the tragic story of Esau. His life seems summed up in this one pathetic sentence, "He sat down to eat and drink, and rose up and went his way." He was not a bad man. He had many fine qualities. But had he sung of his experience as did Deborah, his song would have been a bit like this: "Here was a dish of steaming hot beans until I came; now that dish is empty." What a poor contribution!

Here is another man by the name of Moses. If he had sung after the manner of Deborah what a marvelous poem his would have been. What had life meant to him? It had meant, for one thing, ceaseless conflict and struggle. It had meant bearing on his broad shoulders the burdens and needs of his people. But it had also meant high achievement. "When I began to do business," he might have said, "all these people were in slavery. Now they are free. Now they are on the way to national greatness. Someday they will give to the world a David, and an Isaiah, a Jeremiah, a Saint Paul, a Jesus Christ. But they were only a horde of slaves until I arose."

I

What kind of situation·was it that Deborah faced?

1. One outstanding characteristic of her day was widespread rejection of God. Her people, who had

come to their present position under the leadership of God-guided men, had rebelled against the God to whom they owed everything. The history of the whole period covered by the Book of Judges is fittingly described by three words—"relapse," "retribution," and "recovery." They were constantly turning from God, constantly suffering as a result of their moral failures. Then when things were at their wicked worst they would repent and turn again to the God whom they had forsaken. This was not only the history of the period covered by this book, but it is in a measure the history of the race. Our progress has not been upward in a continuous straight line. Our story both individually and as a race is a story of relapse, retribution, and recovery.

2. This was the golden age of personal liberty. Their complete freedom is declared in this one word, "Every man did that which was right in his own eyes." There were no compelling thou-shalt-not's. There were no compelling thou-shalt's. Every man was a law unto himself. Every man did in every particular just as he pleased. What a wonderful day in which to live! There were no inhibitions. Here was indeed a land where the best was like the worst. Here for once there were no Ten Commandments. "Every man," the high and the low, the rich and the poor, the prince and the pauper, "did that which was right in his own eyes."

3. The period was one of oppression that fell little

short of utter slavery. How different the goal reached by these people from the one upon which they set their eyes. They were seeking to be entirely free. But in their search for freedom they found bondage. This they did not because God lost patience with them and threw them into chains. Their degradation came as the result of natural processes. To such depths were they reduced that the roadways grew up because none dared travel them. They became the plaything of a bullying foe. Even a gallant-hearted man like Gideon had to thresh his wheat in a cave at night to save it from the hands of the enemy.

Why had their search for freedom by the path of rebellion against God brought them to this pathetic plight? Having cast off God, they cast off restraint. Having become separated from God they became divided within themselves. Sin can never make a unified personality. Divided within themselves, they were divided from one another. Group was arrayed against group, one tribe carried on civil war against another tribe. Thus divided and warring among themselves they became an easy prey for the Canaanites that surrounded them. Thus in casting off restraint they dressed themselves in chains.

The experiment made by these ancient tribes is about the oldest and newest in all the world. In the ancient story of Genesis there was a woman who tried to find the freedom of a larger life by violation of the law. Her efforts proved disappointing. Today we have outlaw nations, nations that have no more sense of right and wrong than a tiger in the jungle. The press has quoted Adolf Hitler as making this statement to Hermann Rauschning: "Providence has ordained that I should be the greatest liberator of humanity. I am freeing men from the dirty and degrading self-mortification of a chimera called conscience and morality. . . . . To the Christian doctrine of the infinite significance of the individual soul and personal responsibility, I oppose with icy clarity the saving doctrine of the nothingness and insignificance of the individual human being." But the freedom that Hitler has promised has resulted in bondage to millions.

This is ever the case. The only freedom that man can know is the freedom that he finds in obedience to the law of his being. "If the Son shall make you free, ye shall be free indeed." God has made us for himself, and we only find freedom in him. The fish can only remain free as it obeys the law of its being. If it undertakes to be as much at home on land as in the water, it will not find a fuller life; it will find death. If the bird undertakes to be as much at home in the water as in the air, it will miss the way. If there is anything that history and experience teach more emphatically than another, it is this: that rebellion against moral law leads not to freedom, but to slavery. When Deborah looked out on her world and saw men conquered and oppressed, she knew that they had brought it upon themselves. Nations that fall usually rot down from within. Always when an individual becomes a moral slave, it is an inside job.

II

What did this woman do about this tragic situation?

1. She took it to heart. She could not be indifferent to it. She could not shrug her shoulders and claim that since she was only a woman it was none of her business. She realized that part of the responsibility was hers. She could not rest day nor night for thinking of the desperate sufferings, of the handicapped lives that were all about her. Possibly she felt this the more keenly because she was a mother. In our study of Miriam we said that she was the first career woman that we meet on the pages of the sacred record. Deborah is a woman with a twofold career. She was a home-maker. The name of her husband is given, but we are told nothing of her children. I have an idea that she was not highly successful as a home-maker. Perhaps in spite of her greatness she was not quite great enough to succeed fully in two careers. Few women are.

Of course there are exceptions to the rule. Now and then we meet women of such superb ability that they can be successful mothers and home-makers, and carry on a career at the same time. But such are rare indeed. It is my conviction that the career of wifehood and motherhood is big enough for any woman in the world. If she undertakes successfully to run a home and to run her nation as well she is mighty apt to make a mess out of one or the other. I have known a few very able women to get so interested in outside duties that their homes all but tumbled into ruins. I doubt if any outside success can atone for such inside failure. But whether Deborah made a success of her home or not, I have an idea that she was driven to undertake her task of leadership as a great patriot partly to give her own children a chance. Being a mother, she took the needs of her people to heart.

2. Since Deborah so genuinely cared, she doubtless made the plight of her people a matter of earnest prayer. Day by day and hour by hour she besought God to raise up a leader who would usher in a new and better day. I have an idea that, being a woman and knowing a woman's place, she at first had no thought of offering herself for leadership. But all true prayer is dangerous. It calls for the giving of self. The more she prayed the more earnest she grew. At last she became so desperately in earnest that she said, "Here am I, send me." It is rather amazing to find a woman, even of the strength and moral character of Deborah, chosen for leadership in a crude and iron age such as was hers. But she was chosen because God always chooses the best material that comes to his hand. "The eyes of the Lord run to and fro throughout the whole earth, to shew himself strong in the behalf of them whose heart is perfect toward him." A perfect heart is a surrendered heart. It is one who is willing to take

God's way at all costs. Such was the heart of Deborah. Therefore she became God's chosen leader for that day.

3. Since Deborah cared enough to put herself in God's hands she became a rallying point for weaker souls who dreamed her dreams, but lacked her faith and her courage. Cowardice is terribly contagious. Let one man in an audience be seized by panic, spring to his feet and shout, "Fire!" and it is hard to prevent disaster. This is the case even if there is not a blaze within a mile. But, thank God, courage is contagious also. Let one single soul face any wrong with determination, let one soul set his face with firmness of purpose toward the achieving of any worthwhile goal, and others will rally to him. So it was with Deborah. So many came that she decided that they could hazard a blow in behalf of their freedom.

By this I do not mean that all the tribes of Israel rallied. No leader makes a universal appeal. No cause enlists everybody. Now and then we set our faces to the achieving of a certain worthwhile goal, and we say, "We can win if everybody will do his part." But if that is the only way we can win, then victory is a long way off, for everybody will not do his part. The heavy loads of life are carried by the few. Almost all the worthwhile victories are won, not by majorities, but by eager and determined minorities. If we wait to strike a blow till everybody is willing to do his part we are likely to wait till the close of the day. Deborah refused to wait till all were enlisted.

In that distant day there were some of the tribes that were isolationists. They felt the burden of foreign conquest so little that they were not interested in throwing it off. There were some like the inhabitants of Meroz, who, dwelling in their mountain fastnesses, felt that the great cause was none of their business. There was one tribe, Reuben by name, that was greatly interested. But they merely talked and argued, told each other what they ought to do, and what they would do under certain circumstances, but ended by doing nothing. "There were great searchings of heart," this story tells us. But it all ended in letting a few earnest men go out to the fight alone. It is a pathetic story that is enacted over and over again.

III

What was the outcome?

1. For those who stood aloof, take the inhabitants of Meroz for instance, there was a curse pronounced against them. "Curse ye Meroz, said the angel of the Lord, curse ye bitterly the inhabitants thereof; because they came not to the help of the Lord." This is stern and awful language. We excuse it because we find it in what is perhaps the oldest book in the Bible. We feel that such is native to the harsh, iron creed of the Old Testament. But bear in mind that this grim word belongs no less to the New Testament than it does

to the Old. The sin of Meroz brought a curse in that day. It brings a curse in every day. This curse is not born of the displeasure of an angry God, it comes as a result of the inevitable law of sowing and reaping.

What was the sin of Meroz? They were not Fifth Columnists. They were not spies. They were not traitors. They did not go over to the camp of the enemy. They simply stood aloof. In a day when a great cause was at stake, in a day when the needs of their own people were desperate, they made no contribution. They simply did nothing at all. That is recorded as the sin of sins in the New Testament. The Old Testament stands in the presence of grim wrongs and emphasizes the word "Thou shalt not." The New Testament confronts human need and puts its emphasis on "Thou shalt." In the eyes of Jesus, to do nothing is to be supremely guilty.

To be convinced of this it is only necessary to turn the pages of the New Testament. What was the sin of the man with one talent? He did not use his money to pervert justice. He did not use it to buy the sobriety of manhood or the virtue of womanhood. He did not use it at all, he simply buried it. What was wrong with the priest and the Levite? They did not share the loot that the brigands had taken from the man that lay dying by the wayside. They did not stop to tear from him what small shreds of clothing that were left him. They merely passed him by. What was wrong with the rich man who had a beggar at his gate? He did not have the beggar scourged and driven away. He simply let him alone. It was his selfish failure to help that made his hell both here and hereafter. The life that is self-centered has a curse upon it, not simply in some far-off tomorrow, but in the here and now. The hand that will not reach out to help is withered. There is no sin greater than "to have come and grown and gone" without ever knowing the high joy of serving.

2. But what about Deborah and those who dared rally to her? They were not so well armed as their foes. There was not an iron chariot among them, while the army of Sisera had nine hundred. But these former were fighting in the cause of justice. They were out to give men and women a chance. That happens to be the very thing that God is out to do yesterday, today, and forever. Naturally we are not endorsing all the ethics of this story. It is far from Christian. But reading it in the light of the New Testament we affirm that those who go forth unselfishly to serve are going in the same direction in which God is going. Further, to march with God is to march to victory. This victory is not always immediate and visible. The fighters for righteousness lose many a skirmish, even many a battle, but if we believe in God we can be sure that they will win the war.

There were two factors that entered into this victory. These belong to every victory.

(1) There was the human. God has no way of freeing men, of saving the individual, of saving the world, except through human instrumentality. "I will build my church," he declares. But he does this out of faulty human material. He uses in his great enterprise every woman, every man, every boy and girl, who is willing to be used. The victory here is accounted for in these words, "The people willingly offered themselves." Wherever God can get one willing man, he can do something big and brawny and utterly impossible.

(2) But if there was the human factor in this victory there was also the divine. These won not because they were stronger than their foes, but because God was on their side. Here is a strange word, "The stars in their courses fought against Sisera." Do not get the idea that that is mere paganism. The stars in their courses are always fighting against the man who is going in the wrong direction. This world is built on a basis of righteousness. The man bent on doing wrong fights the very stars. He throws himself in madness against the bosses of the shield of the Lord God Almighty. The final verdict of all such is defeat and failure.

A greater military genius never lived than Napoleon. For years he went from victory to victory. He set his iron heel upon the neck of Europe very much as Hitler is doing today. But in spite of all his conquests he came at last to Waterloo. Why did he lose this battle? Victor Hugo was convinced that he lost it not solely through the might of those arrayed against him, strong and courageous though they were. He lost, according to this great author, because the very stars in their courses fought against him. This is something to bear in mind in these days when despots stalk up and down upon our trembling world. Greed and force and tyranny may win for a day; but in the end the stars in their courses—yes, and the eternal God who flung out those stars—will fight against all such evil and will change defeat into victory.

As this is true in the great world so it is true in the heart of the individual. It was not necessary that Deborah win this battle in order for her to have been a victor. She would have won in her own soul, even though her forces had gone down in defeat. God does not require of us that we win the battle; he only requires of us that we do our best. He says to everyone who dares to fight, "Whereas it was in thine heart to set my people free, thou didst well that it was in thine heart." There is just one supreme and damning failure; that is the failure of having been too indifferent or too cowardly to undertake the battle.

It may be that you feel the futility of the individual in a day such as this. How impossible for you to change the world! But at least by the grace of God you can change yourself, and that will be a big step toward final victory. If you do that, then one day you will be able to look upon some lovely bit of garden and say, "This was mere desert till I arose to farm it in the fellowship of my Lord."

VI

THE SENSUAL FACE

"It came to pass afterward, that he loved a woman in the valley of Sorek, whose name was Delilah."

JUDGES 16:4

HE LOVED A WOMAN." HOW MUCH THERE IS IN that word! What revolutions have been produced by that experience. He loved a woman. We may say that of one man with the realization that that love was like a breath of spring to his heart. Through that experience all that was most beautiful in his soul blossomed into newness of life, while all that was base seemed to wither and die. But sometimes the effect is the very opposite. If the love of a good woman brings to a man's soul the breath of spring, the love of the wrong kind of woman may be a frost, a killing frost. One love may be a veritable gateway to heaven, another may be an open road to hell. It was an open road to

76

hell that Samson found when he fell in love with Delilah.

I

Who was this Delilah that Samson loved? Had he shown the least intelligence he would have known from the beginning that such a love was likely to prove unfortunate, if not disastrous. But there are certain types of men and women who are utter fools when it comes to dealing with the opposite sex. Samson was intelligent beyond the most of his day. But in his relationship to women he was from the beginning to the end of his life little better than an idiot. This love looked toward disaster for the following reasons.

1. Delilah differed from Samson both in race and religion. Both of these create barriers that it is hard to bridge. I do not mean by this that these barriers have not been overcome again and again. But any man or woman who loves one of different race and of different religion is running a great risk. Where love is consummated by marriage it is highly important that those undertaking this high enterprise be of the same race and religion. They need to have something of a common background and a common faith. Samson had a way of falling in love with women who were not only not of his people, but who belonged to a race positively hostile to them. This gave him a heavy handicap.

2. Delilah was a woman thoroughly stained and self-ish. She was little better than a woman of the street.

She might have been, and doubtless was, a woman of considerable physical charm. She evidently knew something of the art of love-making. But morally she was tarnished and soiled. She had an unclean past. She had been fingered by promiscuous hands. She had a filthy present. Naturally with such a woman Samson intended only to play for a while. Having had his fling, he would go on his respectable way. But this was not to be. He made the tragic mistake of falling in love. Therefore instead of his playing with the woman, she began to play with him.

Not only was Delilah a woman of soiled character, but in her we see sensuality at its worst. What she was as a young girl it is impossible to say. Possibly she had been one who had "loved not wisely but too well." Possibly having been disappointed and betrayed, she was taking revenge upon a world that had robbed her of everything. But I think it more likely that her sensuality was not so much a matter of sex as a love of luxury and ease, a desire to live solely in the realm of the senses. To do this she must have money. She must have it regardless of cost. Hers, therefore, was not the role of a woman who sins from weakness, but of one who was selfishly willing to play at love in order to make money out of it. She belongs to the ancient order of gold-diggers. Thus while pretending to be devoted to Samson, she was eager to sell him for a price. Here is womanhood at its worst.

II

Who was this man Samson? In saying the harsh things that we have had to say about Delilah we do not mean thereby to excuse Samson. If Delilah was a soulless gold-digger who was ready to trade everything for money, Samson was still without excuse. He was even more to be condemned than she because he had had so much better chance. In all probability Delilah had never had much opportunity to be other than she was. But with Samson it was different. For one of his day he had had great opportunities. This is true for the following reasons.

1. He was born into a home sweetened by a vitally religious faith. Both his father and his mother were people of deep consecration. He was a child of promise. His parents made his coming a matter of earnest prayer. Before he was born they inquired of God how they might train him in order that he might be the best possible man and render the best possible service to his people. Happy is the child born in such a home. To be thus born is a great privilege. It also involves great responsibility. Samson did not become all that he might have been. But that was not because his pious parents failed to make a serious effort.

2. In love and loyalty they dedicated Samson to God from his birth. The vows of dedication made by his father and mother were accepted in later years by the son. He tells us that he had been a Nazarite under

God from his birth. It was in token of this vow that his hair was never allowed to be cut. A Sunday-school question that used to be asked when I was a boy was, "Wherein did Samson's strength lie?" And the answer was, "In his hair." Of course, this was not in the strictest sense true. His strength was born rather of the vow of dedication to God that his uncut hair signified.

3. Being thus dedicated to God Samson was a man of unusual strength. This strength was largely physical. That was the case because such strength was most useful for the service of his people in the iron age in which Samson lived. Through his dedication God was able to use him as he could not have used him otherwise. The same is true of ourselves. "We are his witnesses of these things; and so is also the Holy Ghost, whom God hath given to them that obey him." As we give ourselves to God, he gives himself to us. Those thus dedicated do not all have the same gifts. The Spirit divides to everyone individually as he will. Samson received the gift of physical courage and power. He was able to do the impossible because of the help of God.

4. For years Samson used his God-given powers for the service of his people. He was not the highest type of hero. We are not to judge him in the light of our modern standards. His story appears in what is perhaps the oldest book of the Bible. But in spite of his faults he was doubtless a very popular man. In spite

of his faults he was the best hope of his people in that dark day. He struck the most telling blows for their freedom that were struck. He failed to follow through, but he did begin to deliver Israel. Though I would not have nominated him, his name stands in the Hall of Fame in the eleventh of Hebrews as one of the heroes of faith.

But along with these good qualities Samson had certain fatal defects. Though he had made a vow of consecration to God his vow was not perfectly kept. In that he is very close akin to ourselves. In spite of his dedication, in spite of the fact that he was called to be judge in Israel, he could never rid himself of a certain moral flippancy. He remained to the end of the chapter a bit of a jokester. He was always too prone to trifle with great enterprises and great issues. He was lacking in that rugged spiritual earnestness without which a man can never be thoroughly great. Then, too, he came to be possessed of a certain self-assurance, a jaunty cocksureness that greatly increased his danger of failure.

In accusing Samson of flippancy we are not basing this accusation upon his love of laughter. His very name signifies sunny. When he was a child there was a sparkle in his eye. Even when he struck a blow at an enemy, he often did it in a ludicrous and whimsical fashion. The turning loose of the foxes with their tails tied together in order to set a field of grain on fire is typical of Samson's humor. He could have accomplished the same result far quicker with his own hands. But this method appealed to his love of laughter. And laughter is good. It is better to have bad eyes than no sense of humor. But Samson never learned fully when and why to laugh. He sometimes laughed at the wrong time and at the wrong things. A man may be quite as sunny as Samson and yet full of earnestness. It was not the sunniness of Samson that was wrong, it was his moral flippancy.

III

What was the outcome of this? It worked tragedy in many directions. Look at its effect in the scene before us.

After judging Israel twenty years Samson decided upon a vacation. That was all right. A vacation when one is tired is just as religious as hard work when one is rested. But when Samson looked about for a place to take his vacation he took it in the camp of the enemy. He thought he would have a better time among his foes and the foes of his people than among his friends. It is always unfortunate when the saints have to play with the sinners in order to have a good time. It is unfortunate when we who claim to be feeding upon manna have to rush off to the leeks and garlic of Egypt in search of a real feast. To have a good time Samson went to the country of his enemies. That was his first blunder.

Having gone to the enemies' country he selected the

worst and most dangerous playmate to be found there. Of course he did not expect to allow Delilah to get him involved. But while she pretended to fall in love with him, he fell in love with her without any pretense. It was then that Delilah saw her opportunity. She determined to cash in on this foolish love. This man Samson had a price upon his head. He was the bitterest foe of her people. She set about at once to gain the reward that was offered for his capture. "How," she asked him, "can you be bound in such a way as to be afflicted?" That is, how can you be bound so as to be brought into the power of your enemies? Any man who had his faculties about him would have become suspicious at such a question. But not Samson.

Here the flippancy of this jokester becomes evident. Here also we see something of that self-assurance that helped him to his fall. Instead of turning from her suggestion with horror he laughs at her question, toys with it, lies about it. With a twinkle in his eye, or perhaps with a loud guffaw, he answers, "You want to know how I can be bound in such a fashion as to lose my strength and become like any other man? That is very simple. All you have to do is to bind me with seven bowstrings" ("withs" they are called in the text). Then Delilah got him to sleep and proceeded to tie him according to his suggestion. Having done so, she rushed in with the horrid cry, "The Philistines be upon thee, Samson." But the giant was not the least frightened. He awoke and snapped the thongs as if they had been scorched in the fire. And to Samson it was only a joke.

But Delilah did not give up. She was still eager for the reward. She knew her man. She knew, too, the art of love-making. "If you loved me as you say you do," she told him, "you would tell me all your heart. Real lovers must not have any secret from each other." Again he laughed and told her that he might be effectively bound with new ropes. But when she tried these, they were as futile as the leather thongs. The third time he came a little closer. He said, "If you weave the seven locks of my hair into the loom, then I will be like any other man." Samson did not go to pieces all at once. No man does. We go up a step at a time. We also go down a step at a time.

By and by Samson had laughed till he was tired. No joke can be good forever. But though he had grown tired of being asked, Delilah had not grown tired of asking. She kept on till he told her, "I have been a Nazarite unto God from my birth. If one were to cut the seven locks of my hair I would then be like any other man." This time she was sure. The hair was cut. Then she burst in with the old announcement, "The Philistines be upon thee, Samson." "So what?" Samson answered. Though he saw what had happened he was not afraid. He and fear had never met. He had won so many victories that he was sure he would go on winning. Samson had even come to take God for granted. "I will go out as at other times, and shake

84

myself free," he declared. But this time his shaking was all in vain. Having departed from God, God of necessity had departed from him. Thus the Philistines captured him and led him away to grind in the prison house.

IV

What did this woman do to him? Or, to state it more accurately, what, under her influence, did Samson do to himself?

1. Through this tragic fall Samson lost his power. As long as he remained loyal to God there was about him a strength that could be explained only in terms of God. But when he broke with the source of his power, he naturally broke with his power also. He went out to face his foes as of old, but this time he went alone. Going thus alone he was defeated and overcome. The same is true in every age. "It is not by might nor by power, but by my Spirit, saith the Lord." When we depart from God, God of necessity departs from us. We then make a losing fight because we fight alone.

2. Through this experience Samson lost his vision. "They took him, and put out his eyes." There is nothing that so blinds our eyes to the fact of God as unfaithfulness. I care not how keen may be our realization of his presence, I care not how clear may be our vision of his face, if we prove untrue, then our faith dies and our vision fades into the light of com-

mon day. There is nothing so deadly to faith as the failure to live up to the best we know. "Blessed are the pure in heart, for they shall see God." To those who renounce this purity God becomes as vague as the shadow of a dream. Disloyalty has a tragic way of putting out our eyes.

3. Through this experience Samson, the conqueror, became a slave. Here is his story: "They bound him with fetters of brass; and he did grind in the prison house." How unspeakably tragic! He was born with a great task on his hands. He was sent of God to be a deliverer of his people. He made a good beginning, but now he is a captive. Now he cannot strike another single blow in their behalf. He has lost his power, he has lost his vision, he has lost his freedom. He has even lost the woman for whom he threw himself away.

But we dare not look at Samson through self-righteous eyes. It hardly becomes any of us to say, "I would never do a thing like that. I could never play the fool after that fashion." Maybe not. Maybe your weakness is not the weakness of Samson. Maybe sin will not get into your life by the same door by which it entered into that of Samson. Maybe it will not be the lust of the flesh that will clip the thews of your strength and blind your eyes and bind you with fetters of brass. But there are other sins just as deadly as the lusts of the flesh—even more so. Therefore it hardly becomes any of us to stone this blind giant. Some of the choicest have gone by Samson's road. You remember that tragic word from Kipling, "When fate wants a man it sends a woman after him, and the woman gets him."

Some years ago I had a friend who was near the top of his profession. He was one of the most helpful and useful men in his church. His home was a delight. I enjoyed its hospitality hundreds of times. His wife was one of the choicest souls I have ever met. But that man began to play a bit. He ended by marrying Delilah. He died the other day. But Delilah did not even have time to attend his funeral. She had to go to the beauty parlor and to give a luncheon to her friends.

> "A fool there was, and he made his prayer
>   (Even as you and I)
> To a rag and a bone, and a hank of hair.
> We called her the woman who did not care,
> But the fool, he called her his lady fair
>   (Even as you and I)." [1]

V

But Samson's story does not end entirely on a note of utter tragedy. Even this story coming out of a long-gone past is fragrant with the breath of the forgiving love of God. In his prison cell we read that Samson's hair began to grow. Little by little the tarnished hero crept back to his old faith. Little by little he returned to God and made it possible for God to return to him.

[1] Rudyard Kipling, "The Vampire."

His enemies never dreamed of such a possibility as that. They knew nothing of forgiveness. But at last this man who had so miserably played the fool came back to receive once more something of the power that he had known in life's bright morning long ago.

Then one night there was a wild party given by the leaders of the Philistines. Everybody was there who counted for anything socially. I have an idea that Delilah was among the laughing throng. As the climax to the entertainment, Samson was brought out to make sport. Having amused the crowd for a little while he asked the boy that had him in charge to lead him that he might rest against the great pillars that supported the building. He had seen that building before his eyes were put out. The boy complied with his request. Then was that grim prayer, and the giant bowed himself with all his might. There was a crash, and wild screams, and then silence. Samson was dead. But "the dead which he slew at his death were more than they which he slew in his life." It is not a Christian story except in this: Samson had come to the place where he was willing to give himself. "Greater love hath no man than this, that a man lay down his life for his friends." And here we drop the curtain over this man who failed so tragically, and who, we trust, was yet saved through the forgiving love of God.

VII

THE GIRLISH FACE

"Would that my lord were with the prophet that is in Samaria! then would he recover him of his leprosy."

II KINGS 5:3 (A. R. V.)

HERE IS A STORY THAT COMES OUT OF A CRUEL AND bloody past. Injustice and oppression were everywhere. Millions of human pawns were being pushed about by ruthless hands, even as in your day and mine. But in spite of all that was ugly and cruel and unjust there were those who found life radiantly beautiful and helpful. Just as centuries later there were saints in the palace of Nero so there was a saint in the palace of Naaman. It is impossible to read this story with open heart without a renewed faith in God and a deeper confidence in our humanity when touched and transformed by the grace of God.

I

"Would that my lord were the prophet that is in Samaria! then would he recover him of his leprosy." Who said that bracing word? Who uttered this longing that is so full of faith and hope and good will?

1. It was uttered by a Jewish girl whose name we do not know. Of this we may be sure, that she was quite young, perhaps little more than a child. The author speaks of her as a little maiden. She was young in years; above all else she was young in heart. These words of brave hope and faith are the words of youth at its best. This little girl not only realized the fact of evil, but she believed that something could be done about it. She was sure that she had it within her power to help. Every youth that is worth his salt begins life with the mad faith that, however wrong the world may be, there is something that he can do to set it right.

In fact, it is just the presence of this high faith that is of the very essence of youth. It is the lack of this same faith that is an infallible mark of old age. If you have lost hope, if you have ceased to believe that the kingdoms of this world will ever become the kingdoms of our God and his Christ, then you are old, whether you are nineteen or ninety. But, if, in spite of all personal and social and national failures, you still believe in a better day so strongly that you are willing to invest your life in a tireless effort to bring it to pass, then you are still in the springtime, whatever the almanac may say. This nameless girl was possessed of that spirit of unfading youthfulness that through the ages has enabled young men to see visions and old men to dream dreams.

2. But if this maiden was young in years she was old in suffering and in heartache. She was a war casualty. She was paying the penalty that people and nations have paid through the centuries for being weak and defenseless. A marauding band from Syria had swooped down upon her helpless nation, and she, through no fault of her own, had been one of the victims. She had been carried away into a strange land. Thus she had been robbed in a single day of her home, of her father and mother, of her brothers and sisters, of every outward possession that heretofore had enriched her life. And to crown all, she had been robbed of her freedom. General Naaman had given her as a slave to his wife. The fact that she was given this position is an indication that she was at once intelligent and beautiful.

3. But though she had been robbed of every outward possessions, there were some treasures to which she still clung. There are values, thank God, that physical force and violence cannot touch. Life can do harsh and horrible things to us. Millions of people in our day have been robbed and plundered both of their possessions and of their freedom. There are many precious possessions that we should like to keep, but cannot. The world with its ruthless force can wrench them

from our hands. This tragic truth our little slave knew through her own bitter experience.

But she also knew through her experience another and a finer fact; she knew that there are treasures of which no force however great and however cruel can rob us. In spite of the fact that she had lost her native land, her loved ones, her freedom, she still possessed other values that made life worth living. In fact, I am quite sure that she was far the most radiant personality in Naaman's palace. She had bread to eat of which those about her knew little or nothing. I am quite sure that the general and his wife, had they known, would have envied her the possession of a wealth that passed all their understanding. I am sure, too, that we also would do well to sit at her feet and learn her secret.

II

"Would that my Lord were with the prophet that is in Samaria!" What does this word tell us about this slave girl?

1. She had a clear-eyed knowledge of the man of whose household she was a part. She doubtless knew his tremendous assets. She knew that in many respects Naaman was a man to be envied. Listen how his story begins: "Now Naaman . . . . was a great man with his master." Naaman's master was a king. Naaman, therefore, moved in the atmosphere of royalty. He was a man of highest social position. He was also a man

of wealth. When he set out for Israel he carried a fortune with him. In addition he was a great military hero. He was held in high honor by his people because he was a victorious general. There was a sense in which life seemed to have emptied all her treasures into Naaman's open hands.

But if Naaman had his assets, he also had his liabilities. The writer of this story, after telling how bountifully life had dealt with Naaman, adds one fatal word. He had all these rich possessions, *but* he was a leper. He was afflicted by an incurable disease. Being thus afflicted, there was a ghastly presence that dogged his steps every time he went into the king's palace. There was a black shadow over Naaman's life and over Naaman's home. This slave girl had not been long in that roomy palace before she had seen unmistakable signs of heartache. She had perhaps surprised her mistress more than once when her face was wet with tears. Wealth and luxury lived in that palace, but so did fear and suffering. All this was known to this slave girl with the clear eyes and the understanding heart.

2. Not only did this girl recognize the presence of tragedy, but she found that she could not rejoice in that tragedy. Who was this man whose every step was dogged by ghastly death? He was the despot who had robbed her of everything. He was to blame for all her woes. The natural thing, therefore, for her to have said was, "Let him suffer. Let him reap according to

his sowing. I am glad of every pang of body and of mind that he suffers. I am glad that he is getting paid in his own coin." But, with a heart like hers, she could not take that attitude. She found it impossible to rejoice in the heartache and tears of those who had done her wrong. She could not meet hate with hate, she could not return evil for evil.

3. Not only did she refuse to rejoice in the tragedy of those who had wronged her, but she actually found herself suffering in their sufferings. Almost before she was aware of it, she was mingling her tears with those of her mistress. She was bleeding through the wounds of the man who had so deeply wounded herself. And because she suffered in the sufferings of her enemies she came to be gripped by a deep yearning to help. Day by day she began to say to herself, "I wish I could help. I believe I could if they would only listen. There is a prophet down in Samaria that through the power of God can cure leprosy. If my master would go to him he might get well. But who will listen to me? If I speak my mind nobody will believe me."

But one day she resolved to speak regardless of consequences. She resolved to do her best, whether that best were of any avail or not. She reached the wise conclusion that while it was not her business to save her master, it was her business to go as far in that direction as she could. How many battles we lose by failing to be thus wise! You have a friend that you long to win to Christ, but you dare not speak because you are not sure of success. But bear in mind that it is not our business to compel our fellows to accept Jesus Christ; our business is to give them an invitation. So this wise girl determined to go as far as possible toward saving the man that she had every right to hate.

"Would that my master were with the prophet in Samaria," she said to her mistress one day, "then would he cure him of his leprosy." How magnificent was such a word in the light of what she had suffered. This girl was a Christian long before Jesus was born. In thus speaking she was turning the other cheek in the fashion that Jesus intended. When he urged us not to resist evil he was not speaking in a crass and literal fashion. When he himself was smitten upon one cheek he did not turn the other. He rather rebuked the smiter. What Jesus was urging was that we act always and everywhere in the spirit of love. When this girl spoke to her mistress after this fashion she was showing herself possessed of the same spirit of which Jesus was possessed when he prayed for his enemies, "Father, forgive them; for the know not what they do." They had robbed this young slave of much, but they had not robbed her of her supreme treasures, faith in God and good will toward men.

III

What was the outcome?

Naturally she at once won the eager attention of

Naaman's wife. I can see this sorrowing woman turn to the little girl with hope and despair contending for the mastery. "Do you mean to tell me that there is a prophet who can really cure leprosy? That sounds far too good to be true. How do you know that it is true? Did this prophet ever cure anybody?" That was a question to which the little girl had to give a negative answer. "No," she replied, "he has never cured anybody, but that is only because nobody has asked him. I am sure that he could cure if he were only given the opportunity."

Jesus indicated years later that she was speaking sober truth. "There were many lepers in Israel in the time of Elisha the prophet; and none of them was cleansed, but only Naaman the Syrian." That is a striking word. There were lepers even among the chosen people. In all probability there were lepers living on the same street upon which the prophet lived. Yet, not one of them was cured. Privilege, you see, is not enough. Opportunity is not enough. A gushing spring at our feet is not enough. We must kiss that spring upon the lips if our thirst is to be satisfied. An eager Saviour who stands at the door and knocks is not enough. We must open the door or he can never be our guest. We can miss life's choicest gifts by merely refusing to accept them.

But this sorrowing wife was determined not to miss her opportunity if she could help it. Therefore, when her husband came home she told him of what her maid had said. The general listened with obvious skepticism, then asked the question that she expected. "Did he ever cure anybody?" "No," came the reluctant answer. "But she is very sure that the only reason that he has not cured anybody is because nobody has asked." The general was prepared to treat the whole matter with utter indifference. "It is all nonsense," he said; "nobody can cure leprosy. Why should I go see this prophet? It would be merely to go on a fool's errand."

But the wife is too desperate to leave the matter there. "Of course," she said, "there is a possibility that even this prophet could not help you, but if you stay here in Damascus and refuse to go you know positively what the result is going to be. You will not be cured. Death is a certainty if you stay here. It is not a certainty if you go to the prophet. Why not, for my sake, give yourself the advantage of the doubt?" Naaman found that appeal hard to resist. But while he was hesitating the words of this slave girl came to the ears of the king. His Majesty was at once deeply interested. Naaman was far too valuable to lose if there were any chance of saving him. He joined his voice to that of Naaman's wife. They both pressed the matter with such urgency Naaman at last had to yield.

Therefore, a few days later Naaman, with a retinue of servants, a letter from the king, and a fortune in money, set out to see the prophet. But, arriving at Samaria, he went first to the king. We somehow always have the feeling that the man in the highest position is the one who can serve us the best. He presented His Majesty with the letter of introduction, which read somewhat as follows: "This will introduce to you my servant, General Naaman, who comes to be recovered of his leprosy." Upon reading that letter, the king was filled with terror. "Am I God to kill and to make alive?" he asked. Meanwhile Elisha heard what had happened and invited the king to send his distinguished guest to the parsonage.

One can easily picture this proud general on his way to the house of the prophet. He pictures to himself what a stir there is going to be when the prophet realizes what a distinguished visitor has come to ask his help. But, arriving at his destination, the prophet does not even come out to see him. Just why he took this course we are not told. I am sure he did it for the general's good. Instead of coming out, he sent some nameless servant to tell him to go dip in the Jordan seven times. It was a very simple and straightforward command. One would naturally think that the general, trained to obedience, would have gone eagerly to do as he was told. But such was not the case. Instead he bristled with amazement, then blazed with anger, then turned and went away in rage.

How human it all is! I can imagine that I meet Naaman a few blocks away. We are old friends, so I hail him. "General, what in the world are you doing in Samaria?" "I came up here to ask the prophet to cure me of leprosy," he answers with indignation. "Well,"

I reply, "did you get cured?" "No," he snaps. "I only got insulted." "Why didn't you get cured?" I persist. "Did you do what the prophet told you?" "No, I did not. He made me angry." There you have it! If getting angry at the church, or at the prophet, or at someone else would cure leprosy, how many would be sound and well who are now rotting down in their iniquities. Too many, as Naaman, try to substitute indignation for obedience.

But why, I wonder, did the general get so angry? To his way of thinking, he had two good reasons. He was angry because the prophet did not cure him in the manner that he had made up his mind that he was going to be cured. "I thought," he said, "that the prophet would come out and strike his hand upon the place and call upon Jehovah; but instead of doing that, he told me to go dip in Jordan seven times." Naaman is not the only man that has missed the way of salvation because of preconceived notions.

Then Naaman was angry for a second reason. It was bad enough to be told to dip himself in a certain river, when he knew so much better methods of curing leprosy. But the crowning insult was to command him to dip in Jordan. "Why," he said, in hot anger, "if it is a matter of dipping in a river, why can't I dip in one of the rivers of my own native land? Why should I turn aside from those beautiful streams to dip in this muddy little Jordan?" You see, Naaman knew a far better way of being cured than did Elisha.

But in spite of all his wisdom he came very nearly missing the way. He would have doubtless gone home and died a leper but for the wise word of a faithful servant. "My father," said this servant, "if the prophet had bid thee do some great thing, wouldest thou not have done it how much rather then, when he saith to thee, Wash, and be clean?" "If the prophet," he continued, "had asked for all your possessions, would you not have given them? If he commanded you to crawl all the way back to Damascus on your sore hands and knees, would you not have tried it? How much rather when he tells you to do something so simple that it can be done by the least as well as the greatest?" Naaman was wise enough to see the wisdom of this word. He went and dipped himself in the Jordan seven times, and "his flesh came again like unto the flesh of a little child."

Why was this? What was God asking at the hands of Naaman? The same that he is asking at your hands and mine. He is asking for ourselves. He is asking for our unconditional surrender. That is the way of salvation, and there is no other. God has no plan of salvation for an unsurrendered heart. Naaman took that way with the result that a few days later there was a new man in the palace of Damascus. There was joy where there had been sorrow, and hope where there had been despair. By her courageous good will this girl enriched the household of which she was a part. She enriched all Syria. She has enriched all the centuries since that far-off day.

Were we privileged to ask her what life taught her, she would mention, I think, two priceless lessons. "I have learned," she would say, "that nothing need rob us of our good will. No wrong, however great, need change our love into hate. I have learned also that since nothing can rob us of our good will, neither can anything rob us of our usefulness. I found myself confronted with what seemed insurmountable evil, but through the grace of God I was able to overcome it. This I have done, not by meeting hate with hate, but by rolling against evil an irresistible tide of good."

If you and I are counted worthy to win the radiance of life's other side, I think we are going to meet some great surprises. First, we are going to be surprised at the smallness of certain ones who loomed large in our present world. We are going to be astonished at how dimly some lights shine that once seemed to light up the whole sky. Then we are going to be surprised more to see the greatness of others that once seemed very insignificant. We are going to marvel that one who once seemed a mere tallow dip is now flashing like a sunrise on a cloudless morning. This slave with the girlish face is going to be among that number. That is what Jesus meant when he said, "Many that are first shall be last; and the last shall be first." That first place is not open to all of us here, but it is open to all of us over there. It is open to everyone who in the face of difficulties holds to faith in God and to good will toward men.

VIII

THE FOOLISH FACE

"Thou speakest as one of the foolish women speaketh."

JOB 2:10

THIS IS A DOMESTIC SCENE. TO SOME IT WILL sound very homelike. A husband and wife seem to be engaged in an argument. The wife has offered a suggestion. As sometimes happens, this husband does not receive his wife's suggestion with enthusiasm. He does not compliment her upon her wisdom and insight. Instead he tells her that she is speaking foolishly. But there is not the hurt, the bitterness and resentment in this word that it has often had when used through the centuries by impatient husbands and equally impatient wives. Everything considered, when Job accuses his wife of talking foolishly he is speaking with genuine restraint and tenderness. What lies back of this gentle rebuke?

THE FOOLISH FACE

I

These words are part of one of the most majestic dramas in literature. The opening scene is in heaven. The sons of God have come to present themselves before their King. Among them, strange to say, is Satan. God inquires of this strange visitor, "Hast thou considered my servant Job, that there is none like him in the earth, a perfect and an upright man, one that feareth God, and escheweth evil?" At this word Satan is tempted to laugh out loud. As it is, he looks at the Speaker with a cynical smile into which he seeks to put a touch of pity. It is easy for him to see that God is allowing himself to be imposed upon. If there is anything that Satan knows it is human nature. He has given himself ample opportunity to know. He has not lived in a cloister. He has rather lived "where cross the crowded ways." He has just come "from going to and fro in the earth, and from walking up and down in it." He has lived with men and knows them through and through.

Besides he has a seeing eye. He can see more through a stone wall than others can through a wide-open door. He knows human nature as none other knows it—not even God. What this keen observer has learned about men is this: they are bad and altogether bad. There is not a good man on the earth. "In fact," says this cynic, "there is no such thing as goodness. Of course, Job is outwardly decent. Why should he not be? He is getting paid for it, isn't he? Look at his big salary, wealth, position, power, children, everything. But does Job serve God for naught? He appears good, but there is no reality in his goodness. If you don't believe what I say put the matter to the test. Cut off his pay and he won't be good any more. Instead he will renounce you to your face."

This word of Satan sounds strangely modern and up to date. We have all met those who are far too wise in the ways of men to be taken in even by the shrewdest. These can read their fellows as they read an open book of very large print. They have found that every man is fundamentally and incurably selfish and mean. To fail to realize that every man has his price is to be pathetically silly. They take a genuine pride in the fact that they trust nobody. Thus they show themselves most like Satan and least like Jesus. Satan is supreme in his mistrust of men, Jesus is supreme in his faith. Denied, betrayed, crucified, he tumbled the responsibility for his Church upon human shoulders and declared that the gates of death would not prevail against it.

The confidence of God in Job is so great that he allows him to be put to the test. Satan is given permission to lay his hand on all Job's possessions. He is only not to touch him personally. Immediately this cynic begins to take advantage of his opportunity. Like a bolt from the blue one disaster after another comes upon Job's defenseless head. His flocks and his herds are destroyed. From wealth he is reduced to want. Then comes the final blow. His children are all killed at one fell stroke. But Job, instead of turning from God, presses the closer to him. Instead of his faith becoming weaker it grows stronger. Instead of renouncing God he worships him. "The Lord gave, and the Lord hath taken away; blessed be the name of the Lord." Nothing finer than that is to be found either in the Old or New Testament.

Once more the sons of God come to present themselves before him. Once more Satan comes also. With a natural pride the Lord asks Satan this question, "Hast thou considered my servant Job, that there is none like him in the earth, a perfect and an upright man, one that feareth God, and escheweth evil? and still he holdeth fast to his integrity, although thou movest me against him, to destroy him without cause." But Satan is just as cocksure as he ever was. "Of course he has not renounced you," he answers, "but it is only because he is so superlatively selfish. It is true that he has lost his possessions, even his children, but the disaster has not touched his own body. Let that happen and there will be a different story." "Skin for skin, yea, all that a man hath will he give for his life." "Skin for skin," that is a suggestive world. It means that a man will strip himself bare of the skin of sheep, or goat, or wild beast; he will give up anything in order to save his life.

There is some truth in Satan's contention. Many men will sell their all for their lives. Near my home in Tennessee there once lived one of the most miserly men that ever petrified his soul by worshiping at the shrine of gold. By saving every penny that came into his hands, by working like a slave, and living like a pig, he managed to accumulate several thousand dollars. He did not trust it to a bank. He kept it always near him where he could fondle and worship it. But one night a highwayman came by and put a gun so close under the miser's nose that he could almost smell the powder. He then asked his victim for a donation. He did not ask him for a part of his treasure, but for every penny of it. And the miser complied with his request. When an old friend called the next day to condone with him he asked, "Did you give it all to him?" "All!" came the tragic answer. "But why did you not argue with him?" "Argue with him?" said the miser, indignantly, "argue with him? I did not argue with him because hell was too close." Yes, all that some men have will they give for their lives.

But in contrast to these there are others who possess values for which they are glad to die. I have known commonplace fathers who would be glad to die for their children. Of course the same is true of real mothers. Then there are countless millions who have been glad to die for their country, for their faith, for their loyalty to the highest and best that they knew. There was a retired minister some years ago who was working for a wealthy ranchman. One night he was taking home to the rancher his payroll, amounting to five thousand dollars in cash. A highwayman put a gun in his face, and made the same request that was made of the miser. But this man answered quietly, "All I have to leave my wife and children is this team of mules I am driving and my good name. If I were to give this money to you, people would never know but that I was in partnership with you. If you want the money badly enough to murder me, you can have it. Otherwise it will never be yours." "All that a man hath will he give for his life." True of some, but of others it is a base slander. All the moral and spiritual progress that has come to us has come through those who possess values for which they are willing either to live or to die.

But Satan is sure that neither Job nor anybody else belongs to this elect company. He has lied and slandered till he has come to believe his own lie. Therefore he hurries away with confidence to put Job to the test. He lays his hand this time upon Job's body. The bereaved man is afflicted with boils from the sole of his feet to the crown of his head. He becomes a loathsome leper, who is flung out upon an ash heap. Here he spends his bitter days and hopeless nights while pain walks with fire-shod feet along every nerve of his body. With wealth gone, with health gone, with everything gone except the woman who has shared life with him, he makes his lonely fight.

II

The one familiar face, I said, left to Job was that of

his wife. What contribution does she make? Let it be confessed at once that her contribution is vastly disappointing. But lest you judge her too harshly, bear in mind that this drama is written by a man and from a man's viewpoint. Not only so, but it was written by a man who lived in a time and place where woman did not count for much. For this reason we cannot regard Jobs' wife as typical. She did not conduct herself toward her tortured husband in a fashion characteristic of women at their best. I know there have been wives who walked out on their husbands when tragedy came. But this is the exception rather than the rule. In my opinion, the wife is more likely to stand by in time of tragedy than the husband.

Some time ago I stood on the wharf at a certain seaport and watched a great liner come into its berth. But it did not make the landing under its own steam. There was an insignificant little tug that clung close to its side and pulled it in. And I have seen not a few men make port at last after a stormy voyage because some brave woman would never let them go and never let them down. Here is one speaking the language of womanhood at its best: "Tell him I never nursed a thought that was not his. Tell him that daily and nightly on his wandering way I pour a mourner's tears, that even now I would rather work for him, beg with him, walk by his side an outcast, live on the light of one kind smile from him, than wear the crown that Bourbon lost."

But Job's wife did not reach this sublime height. Instead the best she had to offer was this: "Renounce God and die." It sounds like a bitter and cruel word. But let us not be too hard on her lest we also condemn ourselves. Many of us have given the same ghastly advice. Of course we have not dared speak thus recklessly with our lips. But we have done so with our lives more than once. We would never dare say this in so many words to those we love. We would never dare urge our fellows to an open renunciation of God. But we often do just that by our indifference and by our careless living.

Decent and respectable wives and mothers have done this time and again. I have known such to get so interested in society that they no longer had any place either for family religion or for the church. If this is sometimes true of wives it is more often true of husbands. How it is that so many respectable fathers and mothers who belong to the church fail to hold their children to the faith that was once dear to them? It is certainly not because they have lectured these sons and daughters on the futility of the faith. They have never openly called upon them to renounce God. But they themselves have renounced him by putting him in a second place. In thus renouncing him themselves they have led to the same renunciation on the part of their sons and daughters. Job's wife gave her tragic advice under the stress of terrible agony. We give ours with far less excuse.

III

Why did this woman speak such a horrible word? "Renounce God and die." It sounds so cruel, so utterly heartless and devilish. Naturally some have looked upon Job's wife as the worst of women. The commentators have stoned her without mercy. Some of them have regarded her as a favorite agent of Satan. Some have looked upon her as a feminine fury for whom no good word could be said. Instead of loving her husband she has become either indifferent or positively antagonistic. She is tired of being worried by him, is determined to get rid of him as soon as possible.

But I think she has been greatly misunderstood. This horrid word that sounds so full of hate has in it no hate at all. It is rather born of deep and tender love. She sees the suffering of her husband, and believes that he is suffering hopelessly. Loving as she does, she cannot but suffer with him. If you have ever loved anybody and watched that one suffer, you can understand something of her feelings. If you have ever lingered without while one dearer to you than life was under the surgeon's knife, you know that the knife that was cutting into the flesh of one you loved was also cutting into your heart. It was not her love that had gone to pieces, it was her faith in God.

Put yourself in her place. The tragic experience through which Job had passed, she had passed also. The wealth that was lost was also hers. The children that were dead had been her children as well as Job's. She had gone through the valley of the shadow of death to lift every one of them into life. Now that Job's health had failed she also suffered in his sickness. She did not see how a good God could inflict such unjust pain. She had come to regard the God whom she once loved as a vindictive tyrant. He is so vengeful that he will strike anyone dead who dares renounce him. Therefore she advised renunciation as a way out. For Job it would be suicide, for her a mercy killing. But anything would be better than the hopeless agony that he was now suffering.

Of course she was terribly wrong. Yet, I am not disposed to be too hard on her. Shrinking from suffering as I do, I am not too sure that I could have faced such a situation more bravely. A splendid young physician in my church found that he was afflicted with a disease for which there was no possible cure. He went home from his diagnosis and took his own life. I think he was wrong. In such case I know I should feel far better about it if I should have the courage to see it through with honor, to stay at my post till the whistle blew. Yet, he as well as this ancient woman did not fail because they were bad; they went down under terrific pressure. But while the woman crashed, Job stood up. "Thou speakest," he said very tenderly, "as one of the foolish women speaketh."

IV

What did Job mean by such an answer? He did not mean that his wife was silly or stupid. Wisdom in the Bible is a moral quality. The advice of this woman is foolish morally. Not only so, it is foolish from the standpoint of intelligence. This is the case for at least three reasons.

1. This woman was foolish because she thought pain and suffering inconsistent with the love of God. For her, faith did not rest upon God, but upon circumstances. As long as the sea of life was smooth, as long as every moment was jeweled with a joy, she thought faith in God was reasonable. But when the tempest was on, when the sea was whipped into rage, when her ship was going to pieces, then to believe in God was sheer foolishness. But Job was wise enough to recognize the fact that pain is as really a part of God's plan as pleasure, that suffering may help as really as joy. "Therefore," he answered nobly, "shall we receive good at the hand of God, and not evil?" Job learned, as millions of others, not only to thank God for their joys, but even more for their sorrows.

2. This woman spoke foolishly because her advice was based on the conviction that by getting rid of God one could get rid of the evil that God seemed to have

sent. Humanity in its blindness has always had a tendency to embrace this foolish faith. At the outbreak of the French Revolution there were those who felt that God stood in the way of their highest freedom. With the cry of liberty and equity and fraternity upon their lips they sought to ditch God. But they only threw overboard those fundamental integrities by which a civilization lives. The same has been true of Germany and Russia in our day. The ends that they have sought have often been good ends, but they have set about attaining those ends by a wrong road.

This same blunder is made again and again by the individual. In one of McGuffey's Readers is the story of a man who so barked his shins upon the grim law of sowing and reaping that he longed for a world of chance, a world where law and order did not reign. It is an old story: when we sin and suffer, wander out of the path and bruise our feet and break our hearts, we often grow bitter and blame it on God. We feel desperately that if we could get rid of him we could get rid of the pains, and pangs, and heartaches that afflict us. But of course such a view is the height of foolishness. To get rid of God is not to get rid of a single sickness, it is only to get rid of the remedy. It is not to escape a single disease, it is only to escape the physician.

3. Finally, this woman's advice was foolish because to renounce God is to renounce hope. "And now, Lord," said a psalmist long ago, as he faced the bewil-

derments and perplexities of life, "and now, Lord, what wait I for? my hope is in thee." That was true yesterday, it is true today, it will be true tomorrow. Apart from God as individuals we are without hope. Apart from God we are without hope as a world. There is a rather hackneyed story of a little refugee girl who was saying her prayers. When she had prayed for her parents across the sea, when she had prayed for the kindly friends who had taken her in, she then added, "And God, look out for yourself, for if we lose you we are sunk." That is everlastingly true. If God has not the answer there is none.

But the answer is with him. In his fellowship both our joys and our sorrows can be blessed to our good. He can change our very want into wealth. He can change our crosses into crowns. You know how a pearl is made? A grain of sand or some foreign object gets into the shell of an oyster and inflicts a wound. Out of the pain of that oyster nature fashions a pearl. So God can do through our pain. So he would have done for this woman if she had trusted him. So he did for Job. At the end of the day he could have testified along with the greatest of apostles, "We know that all things work together for good to them that love God." By failing to believe this, Job's wife missed the best for herself and allowed herself to become a liability when she might have been a blessing.

IX

THE FACE THAT THRILLS

"There was many a widow in Israel in the time of Elijah . . . . yet to not one of them was Elijah sent, but only to a widow at Zerapheth of Sidon."

LUKE 4:25, 26 (WEYMOUTH)

HERE IS A WIDOW WHOSE NAME WE DO NOT KNOW. But what is more important, we know the woman herself. Her face is so fascinating that it thrills us after all these years. When Jesus called her to remembrance she had been dead for nine centuries. The dust of oblivion had by that time buried most of the famous faces of her day so deeply out of sight that they were as if they had never been. But this woman had somehow managed to survive. There was something so beautiful about her that the world was not allowed to forget her. Since Jesus made mention of her nineteen other centuries have passed. During that time countless millions have passed across the stage and made their bid for our attention. But even this vast throng has not blinded us to the winsomeness of this widow. To this hour she brings us under her spell.

Why do we remember this nameless woman? It is not because of her superb beauty. Perhaps she was beautiful. She may have been the Miss Sidon of her day. But if this was the case we are told nothing about it. Neither do we remember her because of the height and splendor of her position. So far as we know she did not associate with the nobility nor move in the atmosphere of royalty. No more do we remember her because of her cleverness. She may have been brilliant, but if such was the case the author considers it too trivial to mention. We remember her because she was hostess to the greatest personality of her time. She was wise enough to know the day of her visitation. She was privileged to have Elijah as her guest and friend. Therefore, though she herself is left nameless, she has been made immortal by her association with the greatest prophet of that distant day.

I

Why was this widow chosen to be hostess to the prophet Elijah? It was certainly not what we should have expected. I am quite sure also that this woman herself never dreamed that such a high honor and privilege would come her way. How then did it come about? There are two very definite reasons.

1. Nobody else was willing to undertake the task.

That is astonishing, I know, but it is sober truth. The people of Israel were a deeply earnest and religious people. The prophet Elijah was the champion of their faith. Yet, there was not a home in all the land that was open to him. Why was this the case? I think we can give three reasons.

(1) Elijah was in bad with the authorities. He had incurred the wrath of royalty. At this time Ahab and Jezebel were upon the throne of Israel. While Ahab was weak and wicked, Jezebel was strong and wicked. She brought to the throne of the land of her adoption a fierce loyalty to her own gods and a savage antagonism to the God of Israel. Ahab was as putty in her hands. The rottenness of the throne percolated through to the lower strata of society. When the situation was at its worst, Elijah came from the wilds of Gilgal and crashed the royal palace. With fine courage he faced these two sinners and rebuked them for their sin. Not only so, but he reminded them that they were going to reap as they had sowed. I can imagine that the face of Ahab went white with fear as he listened, while the face of Jezebel went white with anger.

Having been thus warned, what did Ahab and Jezebel do? There were two courses open to them. They might have changed their ways. They might have ceased to do evil and learned to do well. They might have repented. That is always possible. Had they taken this wise course they would have saved both themselves and their people. But instead of doing this they took the second possibility. They continued upon their wrong road while they grew fiercely angry at the one who had tried to point out the right road. Instead of hating the disease that was working their destruction, they grew angry at the physician.

I read somewhere of a scientist who watched an old savage as he sat under a fig tree and gorged himself with overripe figs. The scientist broke open one of these figs and looked at it under his microscope. He saw that it was literally alive with vermin. Horrified by the sight, he was eager that the savage realize the ugly creatures that he was eating. Therefore, he gave him the microscope and made him take a look. As was to be expected, the savage was at once disgusted and indignant. In fact, he was so indignant that he smashed the microscope to pieces against a stone and went serenely on to eating his figs. Even so, these royal sinners tried to get rid of their sin and its consequences by getting rid of the prophet. Elijah had to flee for his life. The officers of the law sought for him everywhere. Naturally, nobody in Israel was eager to open his door to a man who had a price upon his head.

(2) A second reason why every door was shut in Elijah's face was that the times were so hard. There was a terrible drought. Crops had been almost a total failure. Those who had been in good circumstances were finding it necessary to cut corners and economize. Those who had been poor found themselves facing utter

want. Hunger stalked abroad and starvation looked many a family eye to eye. There were some homes where the prophet would have been none too welcome under the best circumstances. Naturally, when there was a depression, to entertain him was unthinkable. We can often judge the character of a man by what he gives up when it becomes necessary for him to economize. When times get hard, what do you give up? There are those who give up certain luxuries. They give up unnecessary amusements. They may even have plainer food. But there are others who economize on their charities, their gifts to missions, the support of their church. These ancient Israelites economized by refusing hospitality to the prophet of Jehovah.

(3) Then there were those who did not welcome Elijah because they had no great appreciation of him. They hardly looked on him as a prophet at all. He was rather a crude trouble-maker who did not know how to mind his own business. Some of them knew him personally. They would have said with considerable contempt, "I knew him when he was a boy. I knew his father. Why, he used to live up here in Gilgal. You know, anybody from Gilgal cannot amount to much." In fact Elijah was so close to them that they could not see him. In order to see an ant-heap we must stand close to it. But in order to see a mountain we must stand away from it. Elijah was a mountain-like man. Therefore his people were too close to him to see him.

Jesus used this story to illustrate his own experience. Having just returned to Nazareth after having won fame in other cities, the people were on tiptoe of expectancy. They were eager to hear this hometown boy who had gone away and made good. There is no doubt that Jesus looked forward to this service with deep and prayerful interest. He had thought out beforehand the scripture lesson for the day, and what he would say about it. Therefore, when they gave him the Bible he turned to this choice passage: "The Spirit of the Lord is upon me, because he hath anointed me to preach the gospel to the poor; he hath sent me to heal the brokenhearted, to preach deliverance to the captives, and recovering of sight to the blind, to set at liberty them that are bruised, to preach the acceptable year of the Lord."

Having read this text Jesus began his sermon by saying, "This day is this scripture fulfilled in your ears." His sermon, as all good sermons, was timely and up to date. It spoke to the here and now. There is no use to speak to yesterday; it is gone. There is no use to speak to tomorrow; it has not come. The message worth speaking is the message for today. Under the spell of this sermon his hearers for a time forgot their surroundings. They forgot both the speaker and themselves. They were thrilled and uplifted. "They wondered at the gracious words which proceeded out of his mouth." Then the atmosphere began to change. Pride and prejudice and snobbery became alert and alive.

"Why, I used to go to the synagogue with him," said one lusty young man to his neighbor. "He used to make yokes and tables for my father," came the answer. "I went to Jerusalem for my education," said another, "but this man who claims that the great Isaiah was talking about him, never went to school anywhere outside of Nazareth."

Jesus, with his fine sensitiveness, was at once conscious of what was going on in their minds. Every man who speaks with any degree of success has to be able to sense something of what his audience is thinking. "I know what you are thinking," said Jesus. "You are saying, 'Physician, heal thyself. What you have done in Capernaum, do in your own home town.' But this is impossible," Jesus implies, "because you do not trust me. This is the case because you are too close to me to see me. No prophet is honored in his own country." That is the reason that when God needed somebody to be hostess to Elijah he had to go outside Israel to find her. He chose this widow, therefore, because nobody else was willing to undertake the task.

2. Then she was chosen because she was willing. God never compels us to do the big and generous thing. He never compels us to open our doors even to himself. This widow gave the prophet welcome in spite of the fact that there were many good reasons for

her shutting her door in his face. For instance, she might have shut her door because she was afraid. She doubtless knew that Elijah had a price on his head quite as well as those who dwelt in Israel. Not only so, but she knew quite well the woman who was after him. Jezebel was a native of Sidon. She had perhaps known something of this Lady Macbeth before the Israelites knew her. She knew that the strong, cruel arm of this queen could reach out to work her ruin if she found that her home had become a refuge for the hated prophet. But in spite of this she made him her guest.

Then times were hard for her. When the prophet came her way she was looking want eye to eye. That which made her want more distressing was that she had a little boy in her home. This boy was not old enough to work, but he was old enough to beg his mother for bread. It was not easy therefore for her to open her home when she already had such near responsibilities. But it is the burdened people as a rule who take on extra loads. If you want a job done, don't go to the idler, but to the busy. I knew a father and mother some time ago who had twelve children of their own, all of whom were living at home. But when four orphans came to town, they adopted them all. This woman opened her door in spite of the fact that she already had heavier responsibilities than she felt able to meet.

II

Why then, in spite of all these handicaps, was this widow willing to entertain the prophet?

1. She was willing because she was possessed to a high degree of the milk of human kindness. To be kind does not at times require any great heroism. Yet there are other times when it is far more heroic than the daring of death in battle. It was so here. Hunger tends to make men brutal and selfish. Goaded by its torture, the honest may become dishonest; the gentle, savage. But in the face of starvation this woman was possessed of a kindness that was broad and Christian. It was not confined to her own family, to her own organization, to her own nation or race. Those of you who have read *Out of the Night* must have marveled, as I did, at the great loyalty of one Communist to another. There seems no danger that many of them will not face, no death that they will not dare to save a comrade. But along with this there is another something quite as amazing, and that is their hatred and murderous cruelty to those outside their organization.

But the kindness of this woman went out to a man who was of another race. She saw that Elijah was a foreigner, a Jew. She knew how Jews looked upon outsiders as Gentile dogs. But in spite of this fact, because she saw that he was hungry, and thirsty, and tired, her heart went out to him. When Jesus told the story of the unfortunate man that fell among thieves he left him nameless. Had he given him a name and a nationality some of us would have said, "Of course, the Good Samaritan helped him; they belonged to the same organization." But as the story stands, the Good Samaritan helped him simply because he was a man in need. It was in part for this reason that this woman of the long ago opened her door to God's prophet.

2. Then she welcomed Elijah because she was a woman of insight. She was possessed of a seeing eye. She was wise enough to know the day of her opportunity. "As the Lord thy God liveth," she said to him. She saw him not simply as a tired and hungry fugitive; she saw him as God's man, God's prophet. In spite of the fact that he was as close to her as her own door, she could still recognize him for what he was. She did not have to lose him in order to appreciate him. Therefore it was her high privilege to entertain a living prophet. All Israel recognized his worth when he was dead. She recognized and appreciated him while he was alive.

"Seven wealthy towns contend for Homer dead,
    Through which the living Homer begged his bread."

3. She was willing to receive Elijah because she was a woman of great faith. To be convinced of this it is only necessary to reread her charming and beautiful story in the seventeenth chapter of First Kings. On a certain dark and desperate day she had gone out to gather a bit of wood to cook her last meal. As she

was coming from her errand she encountered a gaunt, tired man who made a request of her. "Fetch me, I pray thee, a little water in a vessel, that I may drink." Water was none too plentiful. But the woman went eagerly to comply with his request. But she had not gone far before he called out to her again, "Bring me, I pray thee, a morsel of bread in thy hand."

At that, I can imagine the woman stopped in her tracks. "You ask for bread," she answered through lips white and drawn with pain. "I have no bread. All I have is a handful of meal in a jar, and a wee bit of oil in a cruse. These few sticks you see in my hand I have just gathered that I may go in and prepare this meal for myself and my son that we may eat it and die. And now you come asking me to take it, not only out of my own mouth, but out of the mouth of my boy and give it to you. You are asking a hard thing."

But the prophet was not daunted. "Fear not," he encouraged; "go prepare bread for yourself and your son, but make me a little cake first and bring it forth unto me." That was a terrible test. Don't you think the prophet should have been ashamed to have asked to be served first? A man said to me some time ago, "I was in a home where a widow offered me some money for the church, but I would not have it; she was too poor." Maybe he was right. But Jesus did not seem to have such scruples. When he saw another widow give away her last mite, instead of hurrying forward to take her petty gift out of the treasury and thrust it back in her hands, he was all enthusiasm about it. Why was this the case? It was not because Jesus was selfish. Elijah did not make his request because he was selfish. They both had a conviction that God never remains in anybody's debt. They were strong in the faith that however much we give to him, he always gives back more. This widow so felt the contagion of the prophet's faith that she not only staked her own life on it, but also that of her son.

III

What was the outcome?

When this woman received Elijah, she also received the God of Elijah. Having received God, she received all else that life needed. She found through her own experience what Jesus found in his, that in seeking first the Kingdom of God and his righteousness all lesser needs had been met. This, of course, is not to say that those who dedicate their all to God will after that find the sea of life smooth and "every moment jeweled with a joy." They may have to battle with many a tempest. They may even see their vessels battered to pieces by the crude fists of the winds and the waves. But even these will be for such no more than the rocking of the infant's cradle while they are safe in the arms of a God who loves them and saves them by his grace.

Not only did this woman find her needs met as she put God first, but she became a partner with God and a partner with his prophet. All that Elijah accomplished in the after-days he accomplished in part through her help. In fact, all that this stalwart giant has accomplished to this good hour has been in part due to this nameless widow who dared to give her best in a trying and difficult hour. Thus, through her kindness, her insight and faith, she enriched both herself and others.

Nor is her story unique. What happened to this woman of the long ago is in a real sense happening to you and to me every day. There is never a day in which God does not come in some guise to knock at our door. Sometimes his appeal may come through the voice of conscience that reminds us that we are not all that we might be. Sometimes it comes through the appeal of a friend who needs our help. Sometimes it comes through the clinging arms of a little child. But always God is needing and asking our help. Always, too, he is using those who will allow themselves to be used. Today, as in the long ago, God often has to pass by those who are most rich in privilege and capacities to use the handicapped. But at all doors he is knocking. Whoever opens becomes host to the Highest. Whoever opens finds something upon which to live, as well as something to give to a needy world.

X

THE FEARLESS FACE

"I will go to the king, though it is against the law. If I perish, I perish."

ESTHER 4:16 (MOFFATT)

THESE BRAVE WORDS WERE SPOKEN BY A WOMAN who was queen of the great Persian Empire. She spoke them as she was volunteering for a daring and desperate adventure. Evidently she was a queen not only by virtue of her position, but by virtue of her character as well. The right of the Book of Esther to a place in the Bible has been hotly disputed. Her story seems patriotic rather than religious. But we must bear in mind that patriotism and religion were most intimately associated for the Jews. It is true that the great words of religion, such as faith, prayer, God, do not appear in this book. But in spite of this the atmosphere of the book is deeply religious. The reader is made to feel that God is standing within the shadows

128

keeping watch above his own. We sense his guiding hand in Esther's rise to power and in the courage with which she faced up to her difficult task.

I

How did this young woman come to be queen?

She was not born to the purple. She was not a native Persian, but a Jewess. She was thus a member of a conquered race. Not only was she the daughter of a defeated people, but she was an orphan as well. She had been adopted into the family of a stout-hearted cousin named Mordecai. Her story is therefore a Cinderella story to a superlative degree. If she did not spring suddenly from rags to riches, at least she came with bewildering rapidity from a place of obscurity into the glaring light that played about the throne of the greatest nation of her day. No movie star ever passed so suddenly from obscurity into blazing fame as did this beautiful and courageous daughter of a captive race.

At the time of our story Xerxes was upon the throne of the great Persian Empire. This man had absolute power. He commanded one of the largest armies that, in the ancient world, ever marched into the field. But though big in position, he was little in every other respect. He was a bit of a despotic and capricious nit-wit. We get some insight into his character when we see him decorating a tree with gorgeous jewels because it afforded him shade. On another occasion he is having the sea scourged because it had broken his pontoon bridge. A petty, pig-hearted dictator was Xerxes.

As our story opens this despot is giving a feast. He and his guests have found a unique and thrilling way of enjoying themselves. They are all getting drunk. It is wonderful what insight these advanced people of the long ago possessed. How well they knew the best and shortest road to a good time! As they get drunk they increasingly lay aside their inhibitions and part company with their good sense. The king becomes boastful. His wife, Vashti, he informs the distinguished company, is easily the most beautiful woman in Persia. But they need not take his word for it; they may see for themselves. That they may see, he orders his queen to come before this group of drunken renegades to display her charms. This Vashti flatly refused to do. As to why she refused we are not told. Maybe, as she was giving a feast of her own, she was too busy. Maybe she had imbibed too freely and was too drunk. But I am convinced that her refusal was from far nobler motives. With her training and background she could not display her charms as ordered without forfeiting her honor. Therefore she refused the command of her drunken husband and thus became a martyr to her modesty. She was at once uncrowned and dismissed from her high position.

No other course than this was open to the king, according to the wisdom of his guests. They saw in the bold conduct of Vashti the beginning of a feminine rebellion. They were sure that this rebellion must be nipped in the bud or it would soon spread throughout the whole empire. Soon women everywhere would be disobedient to their husbands. Masculine supremacy was at stake. Therefore drastic action must be taken in order that the nation might be saved. This drunken king, backed by the sage advice of his drunken friends, struck his daring blow. Vashti was dismissed and another queen was ordered chosen in her place.

The method employed for the selecting of this new queen was quite up to date. It was a bit like the procedure employed by the conductors of a modern bathing-beauty contest. In fact I am not sure that the first promoters of this ennobling practice did not tear a leaf out of this ancient book. The beautiful girls of the nation were brought together, the fairest of these, the one chosen as "Miss Persia," was to be crowned queen. Now Mordecai had a cousin named Esther, his daughter, by adoption, in whose beauty and tact and courage he had the highest confidence. He entered her in this contest, telling her to keep the fact that she was a Jewess a secret. Esther won the coveted prize and thus came to the lofty position of Queen of Persia.

II

But she had not been long on the throne before she discovered that high position involves high responsibility. Great power lays a great obligation on its possessor. "I am a debtor," wrote Paul long ago. So are we all. But we do not all owe the same. The greater our capacity to serve, the greater our obligations. Every man owes it to his fellows and to his God to do his best. Esther had to learn that her position was not a privilege simply to be enjoyed, but a high responsibility to be used in the service of others. Her people throughout the empire were in desperate plight. Their peril was her problem. It was her duty to save them because she, of all others, was in the best position to save them.

The peril that threatened them had come about in this fashion. Haman, an able, self-made, and conceited man, was at that time the most powerful politician in Persia. He was a favorite with the king and was able to mold this royal bit of putty to his will. Everybody deferred to him, everybody bowed low when he passed. There was only one exception; that was the Jew, Mordecai. The fact that this one man refused to bow down filled Haman with bitter rage. Instead of realizing that nobody has a universal appeal, instead of being thankful for the rewards that were his and forgetting those that he had missed, he saw only what he had failed to win and forgot his winnings altogether. Thus he was possessed of an inner rage that made him unspeakably bitter and wretched.

Just why he was so bent on having everybody bow down to him we are not told. Of course such an attitude showed that he was very selfish and conceited. But I am quite sure that, in addition, he was possessed by an inferiority complex. This is generally the case of those who are highly sensitive about such matters. The man who is sure of himself can be ignored by his fellows without any great bitterness or despair. If you are perfectly sure of your own truthfulness you can sometimes be accused of an untruth without flying into a rage. If you know yourself to be perfectly honest you can even bear the accusation of dishonesty without having a frenzied fit. It is when we ourselves know that we are guilty as charged that we become most indignant. I have an idea that Haman's distrust of himself greatly increased his rage and bitterness against the one man who refused to acknowledge his superiority.

So great was Haman's rage against Mordecai that he resolved to have revenge. He was not only going to take vengeance upon the man who had offended him, but upon all his kinsmen as well. His hatred for one Jew led him to hate all Jews. Therefore, by shrewd manipulation and by bribery he induced pig-headed Xerxes to make a decree that on a certain day every Jew throughout the vast empire should be put to the sword. His was to be vengeance upon a large scale, as became the big rage of a big man like himself. How it would soothe his wounded pride to bring about the ruin, not of one, but of thousands!

Now, it was to save his people from this disaster that Mordecai made his appeal to the young queen whom he had placed in a position of power. "If thou altogether holdest thy peace at this time," he said to her, "then will relief and deliverance arise to the Jews from another place, but thou and thou father's house will perish: and who knowest whether thou art not come to the kingdom for such a time as this?" Thus appealed to, Esther rose to the occasion. This she did in spite of the fact that she knew that in so doing she was facing great danger. "I will go to the king," she answered grandly, "though it is against the law. If I perish, I perish."

III

What was it that enabled her to dare this desperate adventure?

1. She was a young woman of natural courage. By this I do not mean that she had no acquaintance with fear. It is evident that she was desperately afraid to do the very thing that she had made up her mind to do. The king had not invited her into his presence for many days. It was contrary to the law for her to go to the king without an invitation. Should he fail to extend his scepter when she went, she knew that death would be the penalty. But she did what she believed to be her duty in spite of her fears. That is courage at its best. We may admire the man who has never known the sensation of fear, but we must admire still more that man who, facing a task of which he is desperately afraid, undertakes it in spite of his fears. Esther was a woman of highest courage because, though taunted

by fears, she defied those fears by doing the thing that she knew she ought to do.

2. Then her natural courage was strengthened and undergirded by her faith. She had faith in her people and in the God of her people. She asked that they fast for her. I take it that prayer is included in this fasting. They were to give themselves to united prayer for the success of her mission. There is no measuring the power of such praying. Paul never wrote but one letter, and that to the backslidden church at Galatia, without asking for the prayers of his converts. He believed that their prayers could undergird him with strength and anoint his lips with grace and power. There are few of us, I daresay, who have not at times felt flowing into our hearts a peace and courage that could only be accounted for by the prayers of others. Esther was encouraged to go to her dangerous task by the conviction that her people were praying for her success.

3. She was further undergirded by a high sense of mission. "Who knoweth," said her wise foster-father, "whether thou art not come to the kingdom for such a time as this?" If your situation is hard, if your path bristles with difficulties, if the load to be carried is heavy, that may be the reason you are there. Perhaps God has sent you to your particular field because he needs someone on whom he can rely. Maybe he has put you where you are because he knows that you can be trusted to see the task through with honor. God has a purpose in every life. We need that realization in

times like these. It is a source of measureless courage to be able to look into God's face in times of difficulty and say, "To this end was I born, and for this cause came I into the world, that I might do this particular task and make this particular stand." Esther was undergirded by a sense of mission.

4. Finally, Esther was nerved for her task by a sane view of the facts. She did not make her venture in the conviction that all God's plans and purposes would fail through her failure. God is not dependent for the ongoing of his Kingdom on any one personality. "If thou altogether holdest thy peace," said wise Mordecai, "then will relief and deliverance arise to the Jews from another place." God needs you, he needs me, he needs all of us. But if we fail him, if we turn our backs upon him and become his enemies instead of his friends, we shall not thereby either defeat him or destroy his Church or his world. What we shall surely destroy is ourselves. God needs, and needs desperately, every single one of us, but no single one of us is essential. If this whole generation were to fail him, he would raise up another and march on to the accomplishment of his purpose. But such failure would be fatal to us.

But while Esther realized that her failure might not work world-wide disaster, it would be disaster for herself and for those closest to her. "If I make this venture," she said to herself, "if I go in to face the king, it may cost me my life. But I may win his favor and thus save myself and my people as well. If, on the other hand, I refuse to go, tragedy is certain. Therefore, I am going to give myself and my people the advantage of the doubt." That was a wise conclusion. It may be that for some of us the lamp of faith has burned low. It may be that we have ceased in any vital way to believe in God. If such is the case, I still invite you to venture on him. If you cast yourself unreservedly upon his promises I am sure that he will accept and cleanse and use you. But even if God were to let you down, your failure would not be more complete than if you do nothing at all. Dare, and you may win; refuse to dare, and disaster is sure. Undergirded by this sane conviction Esther made her venture.

IV

What was the outcome?

1. She found favor in the eyes of the king. He extended his scepter. He asked that she present her petition, promising that it should be granted. But Esther was wise and tactful. She knew that the psychological moment had not come. Therefore she contented herself by inviting the king to a feast to be given by herself. There was to be only one other guest; that was Haman. She must have present the great man who had vowed vengeance against her people. The feast was held in due season. To Haman's mind it was a great success. He hurried to his home when it was over with his inflated head striking against the stars. Arrived home, he told of his good fortune. In the thrill

of his triumph he had a gallows built upon which to hang Mordecai. It was fifty cubits in height. He built it on the theory that the higher a man was hanged the deader he would be.

That night the king had a bad time. He was sleepless. But instead of counting sheep he had a book of chronicles read to him. In that book was the story of how Mordecai had saved his life. It came home to His Majesty that this faithful servant had never been rewarded. While the king was casting about for some worthy fashion in which to show his appreciation, he was informed that Haman was without. It so happened that he was just the man that the king wanted. Haman was an inventive chap. He could tell him just what to do to show his appreciation. So the king had him called and put the case before him. "What," he asked, "shall be done for a man whom the king delights to honor?"

Now Haman made the mistake that the conceited are so constantly making. When the king spoke of a man that he desired to honor, Haman said at once, "He is talking about me." Then the vain fellow told the king the things that he would delight in above all else. "If you want to honor your friend," he said, "dress him in the king's royal robe, put a crown on his head, set him on the king's horse, and have somebody to lead the horse through the streets of the city, crying to all the passersby, 'Thus shall it be done unto the man whom the king delighteth to honor.'" Then the king told

Haman to take the royal robe and the crown and put them on Mordecai, and that Haman himself should have the privilege of leading the horse. And so it was done.

From this humiliating experience Haman hurried home with fear clutching at his heart. He and his friends knew that this was the beginning of the end. No sooner had he told his story than a messenger came summoning him to a second feast given by the queen to the king and himself. It was during this feast that Esther disclosed her origin. She told that she herself was a Jewess. She showed how that Haman in seeking to destroy her people had caused the king to pronounce death sentence upon her, his own queen. The king in his rage ordered Haman to be hanged on his own gallows. He is not the only man that ever received what he gave. All of us soon or late reap as we sow. Then because the king could not revoke the law for the extermination of the Jews, he gave them permission to defend themselves, with the result that they were spared. As the Jews celebrate their escape from Egypt by the Feast of the Passover, so they came to celebrate their escape from Persia by the Feast of Purim.

This old story has a word of abiding worth to say to every one of us. We too, have come upon difficult days. We can bewail our lot, we can pity ourselves, and thus wreck our own lives and help to wreck the lives of others. But we can take a braver course. We can face up to the most difficult that life can bring in the faith that we have come to the kingdom for such a time as this. We can put our best into the fight. We can do this all the more eagerly because some of us feel sure of ultimate victory. But even to those who are not sure we say this: "The only sane thing to do is to do your best. If you try, if you face up to life's demands in a brave fashion, you may win in spite of your fears. But if you refuse, if you do nothing, if you merely stand on the side-line and watch the game played and have no aggressive part in it, then you are certainly lost. There is no surer way to disaster than to do nothing. 'How shall we escape if we neglect? . . . .' " There is no escape.

XI

THE AMBITIOUS FACE

"Command that these my two sons may sit, one on thy right hand, and one on thy left hand, in thy kingdom."

MATTHEW 20:21 (A. R. V.)

THE TEXT IS THE PRAYER OF A MOTHER FOR HER sons. In a dingy little courtroom among the hills of Tennessee a young man of hard face was being tried for murder. His mother took the witness stand in his behalf. She was a timid and faded creature, little used to the public gaze. She did not make a good witness, but the prosecuting attorney, who had dealt savagely with the other witnesses for the defense, was as tender with her as if she had been his own mother. He asked her but very few questions and these in the gentlest of voices. At the end he said with a gracious smile, "That will do. You may step down." Then he added as if speaking to himself, "If there is any sin that Heaven finds it easy to forgive it is that of a mother swearing

141

for her son." By which he meant to say that though this gentle old mother had perjured herself, she was still to be forgiven because she had done so for love of her boy. It is on some such ground that we must judge the prayer of this mother of the long ago.

I

Who prayed this ambitious and disappointing prayer? The answer is surprising.

It was prayed by Salome, a good woman who was a friend and follower of the Master. Salome was deeply interested in the kingdom that Jesus had come to establish. Day by day she gave proof of her faith by her works. She was possessed of wealth above the average. When, therefore, she became a follower of Jesus she became a contributor to his cause. She put some of her money into the undertaking. But she made a far more important contribution than money. She contributed two stalwart sons, James and John. There is therefore no mistaking the sincerity of her interest, even though we must confess that this interest was strangely lacking in understanding.

It is not surprising that Salome thought the kingdom of Jesus was to be a visible and political kingdom. In so thinking she was but sharing the views of all the disciples of Jesus. Since the Master was soon to set up his kingdom she thought it well to settle once and for all a question that had vexed and divided the disciples almost from the first day that they had come together. That question was as to who should be greatest. Over and over they argued about this matter. Jesus tried hard to teach them proper views of greatness. One time he had said, "Learn of me; for I am meek and lowly in heart." Another time he had taken a little child and set him in the midst and said, "If you desire to be truly great you must be childlike. True child-likeness is self-forgetfulness." But in spite of this the argument went on.

Now at last Salome is going to get it settled. I am quite sure that James and John consented to her scheme. But they knew Jesus too well to present such a petition themselves. But their mother had no scruples. She felt that she had a just claim on Jesus. Was she not one of his followers? Had she not been for some time one of the largest contributors to his enterprise? Besides this, he was her own nephew. James and John were his cousins. Blood is thicker than water. Why then should she not make her request with every assurance of its being granted?

Though quite sure of her ground she was determined to be very tactful, very adroit. She approached this Nephew of hers and bowed to him as if he had been an oriental king. "Will you do something for me?" she asked. By this she meant to get the Master to commit himself before he found out what she desired. Thus she was presuming upon his intelligence. We have all had such requests. Now and then the telephone rings and some persuasive voice comes over the wire with this question: "Will you do something for me?" Naturally I should like to answer in the affirmative, but I do not dare. Having committed myself, the petitioner might ask the impossible. He might even request me to tell his mother-in-law that she had been with them long enough and that it is now time to go home. This of course would be embarrassing.

Naturally, Jesus did not commit himself to such an unreasonable request. Instead he asked—I imagine with considerable sternness—"What wouldest thou?" Then she came out with it. "Command," she prayed, "that these my two sons may sit, one on thy right hand, and one on thy left hand, in thy kingdom." That is, "When you set up your kingdom I want the positions of supreme honor and power to belong to my two sons. I am not asking this conditionally. Regardless of what you think about it or what anybody else thinks about it, this is what I want you to do for me and for them." How spiritually blind and dull! Salome was quite an intelligent woman. That is evidenced by her gifted sons. But in spite of this fact it was left to her to pray about the most stupid prayers to be found in all the New Testament.

II

Wherein was this prayer an indication of spiritual stupidity?

1. It was stupid in that it was based upon the assumption that a certain kind of position is of necessity

a blessing. "All that is necessary in order for my sons to live abundantly," reasoned Salome, "is for them to have a high position." Of course, such a view was very silly. But countless millions have shared it. When we are miserable where we are, we often fancy that all would be well if we were only in a certain position of which we dream. I am thinking now of a lovely woman who has both character and charm. She has a husband who is devoted, kind, and capable, far beyond the ordinary. But for some reason she has been smitten by a craze for social position. She desires to top the list at the biggest social functions that are given in her city. She is eager that her own parties shall be the most elaborate and the most expensive. She has realized her dream in some fashion. But what of it? In the process she has grown feverish and worried and wretched, while her poor husband has almost a daily flirtation with bankruptcy.

Some time ago I read the story of a donkey who suddenly became rich. He found oil on his farm, and thus became a millionaire overnight. Up to this time he had been a cheerful and contented donkey. But with the coming of wealth his former position grew intolerable. He felt that he must get into high society. He must not associate with ordinary donkeys any more; he must associate with horses. So he went to a beauty expert, got his ears trimmed and pinned down. That night found him among the socially élite. It was a bit of a strain and he was thoroughly uncomfortable, but he went home in the small hours of the morning well pleased with himself. This kept up for weeks; then one night his new friends asked him to sing. He consented, but as soon as he opened his mouth they knew him for what he was. At once his high social position slipped from him. But, be it said to his credit, he did not grieve over his seeming loss. He rather declared that the happiest day of his life was when he got back once more among the donkeys, where he could be himself.

There is no kind of position that can guarantee abundant living. That depends on what we are on the inside.

"The mind is its own place, and in itself
Can make a Heaven of Hell, a hell of Heaven." [1]

Those who win their political ambitions are often more wretched than those who fail. Those who live on Fifth Avenue do not laugh any more often nor any more heartily than those who live on the back street of some quiet village. Yet, madness for position lays its disturbing hand on almost all of us. Even ministers are not exempt. We often have a strange eagerness to be first. This in spite of the fact that some of us have even known bishops that we could not envy. To pray for position, then, is silly, because position has no necessary contact with abundant living.

2. Salome's prayer was stupid because it was so thor-

[1] John Milton, *Paradise Lost.*

146

oughly selfish. Selfishness is always silly. This is the case because, while hurting others, it is deadly to its possessor. "Command that these my two sons may sit, one on thy right hand, and one on thy left hand, in thy kingdom." Why? Was it for the sake of the other disciples? Not at all. Salome had no thought of the rights of Peter and Thomas and the rest. She had no thought of the fact that their mothers might be as deeply interested in them as she was in her own sons. No more was she thinking of the interest of the Kingdom. Of course, being a mother, she thought that James and John were the most fit men possible for the place. But that had nothing to do with her request. What she was asking was this: "Give my sons first place whether it helps on the Kingdom of God or whether it hinders that Kingdom."

Not only did she forget the rights of the other disciples, not only did she put the Kingdom of God in a subordinate place, but she put the will of the Master in a subordinate place also. She called Jesus Lord, but she was not willing to allow him to know more about her boys than herself. No more was she willing to allow him to choose for them. The will of God was of course of great importance, but it was nothing like so important as her own will. The trouble with Salome was that she was thinking only of herself and of her sons. Thus, though she was a woman of prayer, she was selfishly ambitious. It is possible for us to be just as selfish in our praying as in our gambling. Her thought of prayer was one that takes a long time in dying. For her prayer was a means of bending God to her will, instead of bending her own will to that of God. Such selfishness is stupid in that it robs us of all real wealth.

3. Then this prayer was stupid because it was full of conceit. "Command that these my two sons may sit, one on thy right hand, and one on they left hand, in thy kingdom." For what was Salome asking? She was asking that her two sons might share the power, the very throne of Jesus. But she forgot the fact that if they shared that power they must win it as Jesus won his. Jesus, realizing her colossal ignorance, tried tenderly to set her right. "Ye know not what ye ask," he replies. "I am coming to power through suffering. It is through being lifted upon a cross that I expect to draw all men unto myself. Are you willing to share that suffering? Are you able to drink of the cup of which I am about to drink?"

Here Salome turned her expectant eyes upon her two sons for the answer. And they gave it with all the stupid conceit that characterized their mother. "We are able," they said. This they declared when they had little or no idea of what the drinking of the cup of Jesus meant. This they declared though they never uttered a more brazenly foolish word in all their lives. Yet, strange to say, we have taken this word and made it into one of our popular hymns. Thus we often sing as thoughtlessly and as mistakenly as the sons of Salome, "Lord, we are able." Were they able, really? If so, how did that ability show itself? Let us look at a scene that was then less than a week away.

Jesus has gone into Gethsemane to pray. Near the garden gate he leaves eight, taking with him only the three that belong to the inner circle, Peter, James, and John. With these he goes into the inner garden to make his lonely fight. "Abide ye here," he says, "and watch with me." Having said this he goes forward and falls on his face and prays, saying, "Father, if it be possible, let this cup pass away from me; nevertheless, not as I will, but as thou wilt." Then he comes to these disciples, to Simon who had avowed he would never fail him, to James and John who had said so glibly, "We are able," and finds them all asleep. This he does three times over. At last he has to say, "Sleep on now, and take your rest: . . . . behold, he is at hand that betrayeth me." At that black hour all the disciples forsake him and flee, even those who had so glibly said, "We are able."

This word of James and John is one of the most dangerous and deadly lies that man has ever told. If he is a fool who says in his heart, "There is no God," surely an even greater fool is he who acknowledges God and yet tries to live in independence of him. There is a story tucked away in the Old Testament of a people who, mindful of the fact that the world had once been destroyed by a flood, decided to build a tower so high that such a tragedy could never overtake man again.

That is, they decided that they were able to save themselves. "Are ye able to build a better world apart from God?" is a pressing question today. And Russia, Germany, Italy, Japan answer back, "We are able." So do millions in our own land. But such a position is supremely stupid. No man, no group, no nation, can get on without God. "Except the Lord keep the city, the watchman waketh but in vain." The tragic failures of our day are driving some of us back to God as an absolute necessity.

4. Finally, this prayer was silly because it assumed that Jesus was a mere politician or despot who could deal out favors according to whim instead of according to the fitness of the receiver. When Jesus said to Salome, "To sit on my right hand, and on my left hand, is not mine to give," I think she was genuinely surprised. Why could he not give to her sons any gift that he desired to give them? The kingdom was his, was it not? Then why could he not give first place to James and John? For the very simple reason that there are two agents concerned in every gift. Those two are the giver and the receiver.

I have just said that we are absolutely dependent upon God. That is true. But it is also true that he is dependent upon us. He cannot give what we are unfit to receive. I married a couple yesterday. Suppose these had said to me, "We are giving you the privilege of marrying us. We want you, therefore, to see to it that we have the most radiantly joyful wedded life of any you have ever married." I would have had to answer, "That is not mine to give." Suppose I were to go to the public library and say to the librarian, "I want you to see that I get more out of this library than anybody else." She would have to answer, "That is not mine to give. That depends upon you." Suppose Fritz Kreisler were giving a concert. Suppose, further, that he were my best friend, and that I should therefore say to him, "I want you to see to it that I enjoy your concert better than anybody else." He also would have to say, "That is not mine to give."

We need to remember that God is subject to exactly the same conditions. There are multitudes who believe that God could pardon and cleanse everybody if he were not so stern as to be unwilling to do so. There are many who are sure that God could give everybody joy and peace if he were not so niggardly with his gifts. They are quite certain that God could get everybody into heaven if he were not angry at them for their harmless little sins. Of course this it utterly false. God can give only what we are fit to receive. That is true in the here and now, it will be true forever. They that are ready go into the feast. No power in the universe can keep them out. But in the face of those who are not ready the door is shut, and not even God himself can open it.

How futile, therefore, to ask God for what we have no fitness to receive. How blind to pray for a heaven of unselfishness while we are clinging to a hell of selfishness! Believe me, God is constantly offering us his very best. He did so yesterday, he is doing so today. He is saying to us what he said to another son, "Thou art ever with me, and all that I have is thine." But in spite of this gracious word, that son remained a starvling and a slave. This he did because he demanded the enjoyment of the feast while disregarding the conditions for such enjoyment. God's gifts are not arbitrary either to James and John, or to you and me. He gives to all of us the very best that we permit him to give. If therefore we are living lives devoid of greatness, the fault is not his, but ours.

III

There is, then, an open road to greatness for every one of us. We may all share in some measure the power of Jesus. Salome might have prayed for her boys in such a fashion as not to have impoverished anybody, but to have made everybody the richer. It is altogether right for us to pray for real greatness for those we love. It is right for us to pray for real greatness for ourselves. But in praying such a prayer we must pray it intelligently. We must pray it with the realization of the one road to greatness. How did Jesus become great? He tells us in his own straightforward fashion. "The Son of man has not come to be served, but to serve, and to give his life as a ransom for many." And you and I can find greatness by no other road. "Whoever wants to be the great man among you must be your servant, and whoever wants to be first among you, must be the slave of all."

This is the way Jesus won his crown. Listen to the words of Saint Paul: "Wherefore also God highly exalted him, and gave unto him the name which is above every name." "Wherefore"—to what does that look back? It looks back to this: "Who, existing in the form of God, counted not the being on an equality with God a thing to be grasped, but emptied himself, taking the form of a servant, being made in the likeness of men; and being found in fashion as a man, he humbled himself, becoming obedient even unto death, yea, the death of the cross." That is, Jesus became the highest because he stooped the lowest. All of which means that we are great in proportion to the completeness of our self-giving. That is the pathway to true greatness, and there is none other. May God help us to walk it.

XII

THE STRIKING FACE

*"A poor widow came up and dropped in two
little copper coins which make a cent."*

MARK 12:42 (GOODSPEED)

THE SCENE IS THE TEMPLE AT JERUSALEM. JESUS has gone to church. That was his constant custom. The church of that day was at a low ebb spiritually. Many of its members were leading mean and unworthy lives. Its services were doubtless often quite cold and barren and dead. But Jesus never took the position that he could worship just as well outside the church. He believed that he could meet God in the church in spite of the failures of his fellows. He also believed that he could give something to the church in its hour of need. It never occurred to him to try to improve the spiritually impoverished church of his day by merely letting it alone. He made a business of attending church.

At this particular service Jesus selected a special pew. "He sat down over against the treasury." I am quite sure that he did not have to sit there. He took that pew for a definite reason. There was an offering to be received, and Jesus was profoundly interested in that offering. Since he is the same yesterday, today, and forever, we may be sure that he is still constant in his church attendance. In fact, he plainly declares that such is the case. "Where two or three are gathered together in my name, there am I in the midst of them." Not only so, but we may be equally sure that this ever-present Christ is still deeply interested in all our worship. He is interested in the songs that we sing, in the prayers that we offer. He is also interested in the offerings that we bring.

I

Why is our Lord so deeply interested in the offering?

1. Jesus is interested because giving, when rightly done, is an act of worship. During recent years there has been a revival of interest in worship. This is as it should be. We rejoice in this revival, though some of our methods of worship strike me as rather puerile. Some folks seem to think they are worshiping just because they are a bit bored. Then, there are others who fancy that they are achieving this high goal because they have turned off the lights and are sitting in a rather depressing twilight. Somehow I have never been able to see how darkness can be an aid to worship. It seems

to me that the sons of light ought to be able to worship better in light than in darkness. But, be that as it may, giving is a form of worship that everybody might find helpful.

Why is this the case? What do we mean by worship? Worship is the recognition of God as the highest and the best, and the opening of our hearts to him. We do this in all real prayer. This we do when we give aright. As we make our offering we confess that God is the absolute owner of all. We give in the acknowledgment that "the earth is the Lord's, and the fulness thereof." As we make our offering we sing in our hearts, "All things come of thee, O Lord, and of thine own have we given thee." As we thus open our hearts and hands to give we open them to receive. Giving is an act of worship, and worship is about the most rewarding something of which we are capable.

2. Jesus is interested in the offering because our attitude toward giving is a test of character. Tell me your reaction in the presence of an appeal for help, and I can tell you the type of person you are. If an opportunity to give bores you, if it offends you, if you are eager to ride through the world on a pass, then, whatever may be your profession, the chances are very great that you have no personal knowledge of Him whose nature and name is Love. But if you welcome an opportunity to give, if, as those saints of Macedonia of whom Paul speaks with such pride, you look upon giving as a privilege, if you make your offering eagerly

and gladly, then, whatever your faults, the chances are very great that you are a child of that God whose delight is to give, from eternity to eternity.

3. Then, Jesus is vastly interested in the offering because he realizes the tragedy of our failure to give. He knows that such failure indicates that we are selfish and that selfishness is deadly. He knows that to refuse to give is to refuse in any adequate sense to live. He knows that to refuse to give is certainly to lose the very possessions to which we cling with such passionate tenacity. This loss is not the experience of a few isolated individuals; this loss is not suffered simply when the bank crashes or when a depression comes. It is a loss that is universal regardless of how great and continuous our seeming prosperity may be.

Such loss naturally takes place in varied ways. The selfish man often loses his wealth by his failure to enjoy it. There are those who get a real thrill out of money. But this thrill as a rule belongs to the liberal and not to the stingy. For the self-centered man, to spend is often painful. It is too much like parting with a child. Then he loses his wealth finally because the highwayman, Death, wrenches it from his clinging fingers. One moment the Rich Farmer was gloating over his possessions, the next he was as empty-handed as any beggar that ever died in a fence corner. "Whose shall those things be, which thou hast provided?" is the searching question. Well, to say the least of it, they are no longer his. Nor will the wealth to which we cling today be ours tomorrow, unless we make it ours by giving.

Then, often we lose our wealth in a more tragic fashion. We make of it a positive curse. Some of you read a few months ago of a chap in his early twenties who blew his brains out. He had been reared in the lap of luxury. He had never had to make a decision or to stand on his own feet. His millionaire father died one day, and a flood of money swept down over the weakling like an avalanche. The father thought that by building a vast estate for his son he was helping him, but he was wrecking him. Look how this same thing is happening on a world-wide scale. For what are the nations spending their wealth today? They are spending it in killing and in getting ready to kill. A single battleship costs as much as seventy millions of dollars, but when it is finished it makes no contribution to life; it is only an instrument of destruction.

What are we to do about it? Well, it seems there is nothing left but for us to go on pouring out our treasures in an effort to tear down rather than to build up. Through selfishness we have allowed ourselves to be maneuvered into a position where we must defend ourselves against a hostile world. But I am quite sure that had we acted in co-operation with other nations we could have saved ourselves from this unspeakable tragedy. Suppose the nations of Europe and America had been willing, at the close of the first World War, to invest in an effort to build a respectable fraction of what we are now spending to tear down—how different our present might have been! But selfishness is disintegrating to the individual. It is disintegrating to the world. Nothing else is so costly. Selfishly to cling to our treasure is not only to lose it; it is to change it into a curse. No wonder, therefore, that Jesus looks with anxious interest when the offering is being received.

4. Again, Jesus is interested in our giving because he knows how vastly helpful it may be. Money is not a cheap and worthless something. Money is condensed energy, it is pent-up power. While it can be made into a curse, it can become an unspeakable blessing. It can buy food for the hungry and clothing for the naked. It can also open doors of opportunity to the underprivileged. It can be enlightenment for the ignorant. It can build homes, colleges, and universities. If it can help to make the world a hell, it can also help to make it a heaven.

By our money we can help to build the Church of the living God. Jesus was interested in the Church in the long ago; he is interested in it still. He believed in it so strongly that he poured the wealth of his life into the building of it. He saw in it the one hope of the world. If it was needed in the long ago it is needed even more desperately today. The despotisms of Europe are working havoc in many ways. But their deadliest blows are being struck against the worth of personality. For them, the state is all, the individual is nothing. If we are to keep alive in our land a sense of the supreme worth of personality, we cannot do this by battleships and standing armies. We must by the giving of our substance and ourselves keep vital and strong the Church of the living God.

5. Finally, Jesus is interested in our giving not only because he is interested in the object for which we give, but because he is interested in ourselves. He knows that giving not only enriches others, but it enriches the giver even more. That is what Jesus meant when he said, "It is more blessed to give than to receive." It is a great privilege to receive. We have all enjoyed that privilege. But finer still is the privilege of giving. This is the case because giving enables us to do something that is Godlike. It is by giving that we put meaning and purpose into our getting. It is by giving that we change what would be an inevitable curse into an unspeakable blessing. No wonder then that Jesus is vastly interested in the offering.

II

What did the Master see as he sat over against the treasury?

Strange to say, it would seem that he saw nothing that was ugly and mean. Knowing human nature as we do, we find this a bit surprising. It would not have been astonishing if the story had read like this: "Jesus sat over against the treasury and saw how a certain man of nimble fingers stole money from the treasury." More likely still would have been this word: "Jesus sat over against the treasury and saw how certain men of great capacity gave only a shameful fraction of what they ought to have given, while others gave nothing at all." But if there was a single shameful and disgraceful deed done that day it is not mentioned. What then did Jesus see?

1. He saw a multitude casting money into the treasury. Splendid! There was a vast congregation. Not only so, but it would seem that everyone brought an offering. If such was not the case, it ought to have been. Giving, I repeat, is an act of worship. Therefore everybody ought to enjoy that enriching experience. Everybody ought to relate himself in some fashion to the financial program of his church. That is reasonable; that is scriptural. "Upon the first day of the week let every one of you lay by him in store, as God hath prospered him." We are sure, therefore, that Jesus looked with glad eyes as this multitude cast their gift into the treasury.

2. A second great sight that he saw was this: "Many that were rich cast in much." Then there were rich men in that far-off day who came to church, as there are such today. Naturally these men were very busy. They were carrying heavy loads. But they were not so busy that they had to sleep all through the Sabbath. They were not so busy that they had to give the day to golf. They were not so busy that they had to give dinners on the Sabbath evening at the Country Club. In spite of the heavy burdens they carried they came to

church. This fact is to their credit. It is not easy for a rich man to be vitally religious. This is not my word; it is the word of Jesus. "How hardly shall they that have riches enter into the kingdom of God!" Of course most of us are willing to run the risk. But every man who has lived and observed knows the profound truth of this statement. It is hard for a rich man to enter into the Kingdom or to remain in the Kingdom for at least two very obvious reasons.

It is hard, in the first place, because money lays such a heavy claim upon the attention of its possessor. If we are rich we have to keep close watch upon our possessions or they will slip through our hands. Money is sometimes hard to get; often it is yet harder to keep. Because of this it tends to rivet our attention. We fix our gaze upon it as the man with the muckrake in Bunyan's immortal story fixed his gaze upon the dirt and sticks and straw of the barnyard. Thus watching our money we often come to love it. Thus allowing it to fill such a large place in our hearts we have no time for prayer, Bible reading, church attendance, those exercises that help to keep alive in our hearts a sense of God.

Then a rich man finds it hard to be a Christian because money so often gives a false sense of independence. Money does possess a certain kind of power. It often gives a sense of security. It makes one feel independent of his fellows. Do you recall that rich young man who declared that the reason for his eagerness for more money was in order that he might tell his fellows to go to hell? By this he simply meant that he wanted to be independent so far as other men were concerned. Often this feeling of independence toward men marks also the attitude of the rich man toward God. It is not easy to pray with fervor, "Give us this day our daily bread," even if one has as much as a hundred thousand dollars in the bank. Therefore, since riches tend to give their possessor a sense of independence even toward God, they are very dangerous. This is the case because independence toward God makes vital religion impossible. In fact it is the very fountain source of all sin.

3. But while Jesus looked with gladness upon this multitude of givers, he saw one giver that thrilled him above all others. He saw a poor widow drop in two little copper coins that make a cent. At this Jesus fairly leaped to his feet in glad enthusiasm. He saw that this woman towered above her fellows as a tall pine tree might tower above the shrubbery at its roots. So thrilled was he that he must share his enthusiasm with his friends. So he called these friends and pointed her out, saying, "This poor widow hath cast more in, than all they which have cast into the treasury."

III

How absurd! Such a statement seems little short of ridiculous. How can it be true? Naturally it was not more in intrinsic worth. Wherein then, I repeat, was this declaration of the Master true?

1. Her gift was great in its devotion. She gave not because she was seeking the approval of her fellows. I dare say there was not one present who had insight enough to appreciate her gift with the exception of Jesus. She gave because the love in the heart of her made it impossible for her to refrain from giving. Love is like that. It will do the big thing if it can. If it cannot, it will do the little thing in a grand way. Her gift was great because there was great love in it. Two mites are very insignificant in themselves, but when to them is added the love of a devoted heart the result is a treasure of unspeakable value. Because there was so much love back of this gift Jesus could not but greet it with great enthusiasm.

2. Then her gift was great because it was shot through with the spirit of the Cross. How did Jesus give? He gave with abandon. He gave his all. He gave till he had nothing left. "Being in the form of God he thought not equality with God a thing to be clung to, but he emptied himself." He gave himself utterly. So did this woman. "These others," said Jesus, "have given out of their abundance. What they have left is amply sufficient. Having given they will still have to deny themselves of nothing." But the gift of this woman is great because it has in it the very spirit of Calvary. No wonder Jesus was thrilled by it.

3. Finally, this gift has become the largest in terms

of dollars and cents. There is no measuring what God can do with those values that look smallest and most insignificant in the eyes of men. How many millions, both rich and poor, have been heartened to give by this beautiful story! The two little copper coins of this widow have through the centuries become mighty magnets that have drawn to them a stream of wealth beyond all power to estimate. There is no doubt that while the large gifts of the rich proved helpful, far and ahead the most enriching gift that day was that of this poor widow. Literally she cast more in than all they that did cast into the treasury.

IV

What has this story to say to you and me?

1. It gives us a bit of understanding of the privilege of giving. It tells us that giving is not only a privilege, but a necessity. Because this is the case every one of us ought to have some plan for giving. This matter of giving is far too important for us to treat it in the haphazard fashion in which so many of us do treat it. The majority of church people have no technique for giving at all. They give at odd intervals, sometimes in the middle of the year, at other times at the end. They have no set times. Then they often give from no fixed principles. They give if they are approached by the right person. They give if their emotions are stirred. They give if they like the pastor. But, wanting in tech-

nique, they miss in a large measure the privilege of helping and being helped by their giving.

2. Our giving, to reach its best, must have in it something of the whole-hearted devotion of this woman. By this I do not mean that we are commanded to give away all our possessions. What we are to give is ourselves. We are to dedicate our lives to God. In the dedication of ourselves we naturally also dedicate our possessions. If we do this we shall not give away all that we have, but we will use our wealth not as its owners, but as its possessors. We shall act conscientiously as the good stewards of Jesus Christ. We shall give our money as we give ourselves under the leadership of the Divine Spirit.

3. Finally, this thrilling story tells us that the place of highest usefulness is equally within the reach of all of us. It is not the quantity of our gifts that counts, but the quality. Who will be the largest contributor to our church this year? It may be the one who gives the most in terms of dollars and cents. It may also be the one who gives the least. Whoever gives most in fidelity, in consecration, in whole-hearted love, that one is the largest giver in the eyes of Him who sees us and knows us for what we are.

XIII

THE WORRIED FACE

"Martha, Martha, you are anxious and wor-
ried about a multitude of things."

LUKE 10:41 (WEYMOUTH)

THIS SCENE IS SO HOMELIKE THAT IT DOES NOT take much imagination to reconstruct it. We see it so clearly that we almost feel as if we had been present in person. It takes place in one of the well-to-do homes of Bethany. This home is famous for its hospitality. In all the land, I am sure, there was no other home that gave Jesus quite so warm a welcome. I can well imagine that he often traveled miles out of his way, even under the burden of great weariness, to get to enjoy the hospitality offered him by this select circle of friends, Martha, Mary, and Lazarus. When opposition began to gather and other doors were shut in his face, this one was always open.

Today Jesus has exercised the privilege of friendship

at its best. He has dared to come to this home unannounced. That is a sharp test. When our friends say to us, "Just drop in any time. Come out any day and take pot luck with us," they usually mean that we are not to come at all. Generally speaking, any time is equivalent to no time. Those who are really serious in giving invitations usually specify the day and the hour. Their failure to be specific simply means that they desire to make an impression of this type of friendliness without taking the trouble to be friendly. It takes a very rash visitor, therefore, or one who is very confident, to come to dinner unannounced. But Jesus did just that.

The reason that we are so sure he was not expected is that preparations for his entertainment had to be made after his arrival. Martha, who was the head of the house, had hardly greeted her Guest before she excused herself to hurry away into the kitchen. Mary doubtless went also, at least for a little while. The story reads, "She had a sister called Mary, who also sat at the Lord's feet, and heard his word." That word "also" implies that she did not spend her entire time sitting at the feet of Jesus and listening to his conversation. She helped a bit with the preparations. But soon she came back from the kitchen and left Martha to carry on alone. Mary thought that the dinner was important, but she did not think it of supreme importance. Hence she took her place at the feet of her Guest to hear his word.

Martha carried on alone for a while with her usual efficiency. Then she began to get annoyed that Mary did not return. More than once she looked from the kitchen door with flushed face and angry eyes. But neither Mary nor the Master saw her. At last the volcano that has been smoldering in her heart makes an eruption. She hurries out of the kitchen to explode upon the company. "Master," she asks indignantly, "is it all one to you that my sister has left me to serve alone? Bid her that she help me." It is quite evident that Martha's patience is worn threadbare. She feels that she is being mistreated. For this reason, she is quite sure that her Guest is going to take sides with her and rebuke her sister for her neglect. But instead of rebuking Mary he rebukes Martha. There is no shutting our eyes to this fact, however much we may sympathize with Martha. With great tenderness Jesus answers her as he might have answered a fretting child, "Martha, Martha, you are anxious and worried about a multitude of things."

I

Why does Jesus rebuke Martha?

It is certainly not because Martha is a woman of practical turn of mind. It is all to the good that she has a way of looking facts in the face. Even as she stands with Jesus beside her brother's grave she does not lose her head. She is still possessed of what we are accustomed to regard as practical common sense. Therefore, when the Master asks that the stone be removed from the mouth of the grave, Martha reminds him how long her brother has been dead, and that by now decomposition has set in. Martha believes in keeping her feet on the ground. She believes in ministering to the physical needs of people. She believes in good food. She perhaps has the reputation of being the best cook in Bethany. She knows that to prepare a good dinner fit for such a Guest as hers requires work. An exceedingly practical woman is Martha; and that, I repeat, is all to the good.

But it so happens that this Guest is quite as practical as Martha. In fact, he is far more so. While he never forgot that men have bodies he constantly remembered that they have souls as well. He was always concerned with the physical needs of men, but not with these needs only. He too believed in hard work—quite as much as Martha. One detects a note of pride in his declaration, "My Father worketh even until now, and I work." The Kingdom that Jesus came to set up does not fit into some imaginary world; it fits into this world that we know. When Jesus, therefore, rebukes Martha it is not because she is too practical. The fact is, she is not practical enough. He is not blaming her for trying to put through her task in what seems to her a sane and common-sense fashion.

No more is Jesus rebuking Martha because she is lacking in kindness. Martha is the very embodiment of kindness. I dare say she has more good deeds to her credit than any other woman in Bethany. Had you talked to the mothers who lived in her village, one of them would have told you that when her little Benjamin was sick Martha could do more with him than anybody else. He would sleep on her lap when he could sleep nowhere else. He would take medicine from her hand when all others had failed. When grown-ups had passed through lean, gray days, when their appetites had failed, when the most palatable dishes nauseated, they could eat food prepared by Martha's skilled hands. In fact, we may be sure that deeds of weekday holiness were constantly falling from her hands as noiselessly as the snow. Martha is kind.

No more is Jesus rebuking Martha because of her lack of love and loyalty to himself. She is his devoted friend. As the head of the family it was she who gave him welcome into this home. The writer of the Fourth Gospel declares that Jesus loved Martha, and her sister, and Lazarus. Martha is put first. The warm place she had in the heart of the Master is an indication of the secure place that her Master held in her heart. This kind, practical Martha would have gladly died for her Guest, yet he finds it necessary to rebuke her. Why, I repeat, is this the case?

He is not rebuking her because she is a practical worker, not because she is lacking either in kindness or love or loyalty. He is rather rebuking her for being worried. "You are anxious and worried," he says, "about a multitude of things." Jesus was a constant foe of worry. He knew the futility of it. He knew the evil of it. He knew how it spoils life. Therefore, he asks, "Which of you by taking thought can add one cubit unto his stature?" "Take therefore no thought for the morrow," he warns, "for the morrow shall take thought for the things of itself." Paul doubtless had this word in mind when he wrote, "In nothing be anxious." Jesus and all who share his mind look at worry as a hurtful and deadly foe. There is nothing but rebuke, therefore, in this word of Jesus, "Martha, Martha, you are anxious and worried."

II

Why was Martha worried? Had you slipped into that tempestuous kitchen and said to this hot and flustered woman, "Steady now, Martha, don't get worried, don't be upset," she would doubtless have turned upon you and given you a piece of her mind. She would have been more explicit even than she was when she exploded in the drawing-room. "Why shouldn't I worry? I have enough to worry anybody." She really thought she was telling the truth. She did not realize, as all of us ought to realize, that worry comes from the inside, not from the outside. But what was worrying her?

1. She was worried about the dinner. She was entertaining an honored guest. She wanted to please that guest above all else. She desired to make his visit just as delightful as possible. But she felt that this would be impossible unless the dinner was correct in every de-

tail. But how could it be correct when the fire was giving off more smoke than heat? How could it be when the bread was not rising? How could it be when the cake was going to be sadder than any funeral? How could it be when she had to look after everything while Mary looked after nothing? Martha was worried because she was afraid that the dinner was going to be a flop.

2. If the dinner worried Martha, Mary worried her still more. She was deeply devoted to this lovable sister of hers. But Mary could be very annoying at times, and this was one of the times. She could be so silly, so utterly impractical. "Doesn't she know that folks have to eat?" Martha is muttering to herself. "Doesn't she realize that a dinner does not cook itself?" But her grumbling went for nothing. Yet, while one dish seemed not to be cooking at all, while another was burning, this dreamy sister of hers went right on listening to the Master as if she didn't have a care in the world and as if all one had to do to produce a feast was just naked nothing. By and by Martha got so worried that she became positively fretful and angry. She would have quarreled with her if Mary had been willing to quarrel back at her. Martha was worrying over Mary.

3. Strangest of all, Martha was worried over Jesus. How unbelievable! and yet how tragic! This should have been a red-letter day in the life of Martha. She has as her guest one who, according to her own con-

fession, is the Christ of God. She is entertaining him who is the Resurrection and the Life. But she does not enjoy him. She does not take time to sit at his feet and drink in his wisdom. Instead she is more fretful and peevish than she would have been had Jesus not come. Such a story would be unbelievable if it had not been repeated in so many of our lives. But for us the fact of God revealed in Christ is often more weight than wings. Our religion sometimes annoys us more than it gladdens and helps us. Here then is Martha worrying over her dinner, over her sister, and even over Jesus. No wonder that her devoted Friend finds it necessary to rebuke her.

III

But why should not Martha worry? What is the harm of it? Why is Jesus so against it? We can get some insight into the answer to these questions by seeing what worry did for this good woman on this occasion.

1. It spoiled the day for Martha. She should have been the happiest woman in Bethany. But instead she was one of the most unhappy. It took a lot of sheer wretchedness to cause this woman, who was naturally so kind, to criticize her sister and her Guest. Then, having uttered this criticism, she became more miserable still. She who was the very embodiment of kindness and consideration had been unkind to the ones that she loved the most. With what penitence and shame she

must have gone about the further preparation of that dinner! Then, when it was all ready, I have an idea that it was about the poorest dinner that Martha ever cooked. I am sure of this because worry is not conducive to good work of any kind. We can perform any task better when we have inward peace. This dinner was in all probability a poor affair. But even if it were good Martha would have been too worried to enjoy it. Thus does worry hurt the one who worries. It hurts our work. Worry is killing. If we persist in it long enough it lays waste life.

2. But the evil of Martha's worry did not stop with herself. Her worry made her hard to live with. She not only spoiled the day for herself, but she seems to have done her best to spoil it for others. This we who worry can often do without trying. Martha made it hard on Mary. While Mary sat at the feet of Jesus she had no thought of annoying her devoted sister. She had no thought of anything except the Guest whom she loved. She was evidently a choice and tender soul. How grieved therefore she must have been when she found that she had worried Martha! How embarrassed she must have been when her sister so far forgot herself as to rebuke not only herself, but their Guest as well. Thus those who worry not only hurt themselves, but they hurt others as well.

3. Finally, Martha, through her worry, grieved and disappointed Jesus. The skies above the head of her Friend were growing black with the storm-clouds of

opposition. The outside world was full of turmoil, confusion, and hostility. From out this driving storm Jesus had come to Martha's house for a day of quiet rest. He had come here because he was sure of his welcome. But having come, he could not fail to see that he was hindering rather than helping. Even though he knew that he was welcome, he knew also that he was proving a source of annoyance. He was upsetting about the best friend he had in the world. There is therefore tender grief in the heart of Jesus as he rebukes Martha. Thus, when we worry we hurt ourselves, we hurt our fellows, we grieve and disappoint our Lord.

IV

To this I think we are all ready to agree. But some may ask half-fretfully, "What are we to do about it? How can we help worrying in a world like this and in times like these? How can we help worrying in a situation like ours? How can we keep from worrying when there are so many things that can lay waste our lives and break our hearts? We are so sensitive. We can be so sorely wounded, not only through the tragedies that come to us personally, but through those that come to the ones we love. Yet Jesus lived above worry, and calls upon us to do the same. Mary was living above it as she thus sat at the feet of Jesus. What suggestions for victory can we offer?

1. We must realize that the conquest of worry does not depend upon our circumstances. There are those who are going to quit worrying as soon as they find themselves in a better situation. As soon as they pay the last installment on their home or on their car, as soon as they recover from their last attack of illness, as soon as their income reaches a certain figure, then they are going to be through with worry. So Martha thought. She said, "As soon as I am perfectly sure that the bread is going to turn out all right, that the cake is going to be perfect, that the roast is going to be all that it should be, that the dinner is to be the best ever served, then I am going to stop worrying and be at peace. But Mary, living in the same home, sharing the same responsibilities, as eager to please the Master as Martha, did not share her feverish anxiety. Some of you did not sleep last night, not because the bed was uncomfortable, but because you were worried. Nor was your worry born of the fact that life has dealt more harshly with you than with others. There are those living on your street who are in circumstances far worse than yours, yet these are enjoying a peace that passeth understanding.

2. We may help ourselves by a wise tolerance. This would certainly have helped Martha. We may assume that she and Mary were equally devoted to Jesus. Martha had a very definite and practical way of expressing her devotion. She was eager to prepare him a good dinner, to make a proper feast in his honor. But

Mary was wise enough to know that Jesus would enjoy sympathy, understanding, and appreciation even more than he would enjoy an elaborate dinner. Therefore, after she had done a bit of work, she sat at his feet and listened to his conversation. This worried and angered Martha. She thought that, because Mary did not serve just as she served, she was making no contribution at all. We are often like that. Even the beloved disciple, John, got terribly worried once because he saw a man who was not of his company casting out demons. We are likely to worry less if we exercise a wise tolerance. Thus we shall recognize that good in others that is different from our own. That is what Paul meant when he said, "If there be any virtue, and if there be any praise, think on these things."

3. If we are to avoid worry we must put things in their right place. Martha worried because she allowed things to get in the saddle. One of the saddest tyrannies of our day is the tyranny of things. Martha was deeply devoted to Jesus. She was preparing this feast out of sheer love. But she became so concerned about the secondary that she forgot the primary. She became so worried about her dinner that she largely forgot her Guest. That is a danger that is far more pressing in our hectic day than in the long ago. It is easy for the best of us to become so concerned about holy things that we forget the holy Lord. But whenever things, however important, get into first place, one

result is worry. To conquer anxiety we put things in their right place.

4. Finally, to conquer worry we must put Christ in his right place. That is how Mary won the victory. She realized that while Jesus desires our gifts he desires yet more, our love and our fellowship. He seeks not our service primarily, he seeks ourselves. Mary sat at his feet, listened to his conversation, entered into fellowship with him. She put Christ first. Hers was the highest and holiest form of prayer, the prayer of communion. Such prayer makes worry impossible.

Anxiety and a sense of God cannot live in the same heart. "The Lord of hosts is with us; the God of Jacob is our refuge." This then follows as naturally as night follows day: "Therefore will we not fear though the earth do change, and though the mountains be shaken into the heart of the seas." I read somewhere of an aviator who was making a flight around the world. He spent a night at a certain airdrome in Arabia. Some hours after he had taken off the next morning he heard a noise in his airplane that he recognized as the gnawing of a rat. He realized with horror that while his ship was grounded this enemy had entered, with results that might prove disastrous. He did not know what bit of his airplane those sharp teeth were cutting. He did not know what moment this gnawing might precipitate a crash. But what was he to do? He was too far from the port from which he had taken off to return. The next landing base was hours ahead.

His helplessness made his blood run cold. Then he remembered that the rat was a rodent, that he was a creature that lived on the earth and under the earth. He was not made for the heights. Therefore, he began to climb. He went up a thousand feet, then another thousand, then another. By and by he was far above the clouds. Then the gnawing hushed as suddenly as it had begun. When the aviator landed in safety at the next airdrome, he found a dead rat in the pit of his plane. And worry cannot live in the fellowship that Mary enjoyed. That is what Paul meant when he said, "In nothing be anxious; but in everything by prayer and supplication with thanksgiving let your requests be made known unto God. And the peace of God, which passeth all understanding, shall keep your hearts and minds through Christ Jesus." That is the offer of Jesus himself: "Peace I leave with you, my peace I give unto you: not as the world giveth, give I unto you. Let not your heart be troubled, neither let it be afraid."

XIV

THE BEAUTIFUL FACE

"She has done a beautiful thing to me."

MARK 14:6 (MOFFATT)

HERE IS A STORY THAT WILL LIVE FOREVER. IT IS too fascinating, too winsome ever to be forgotten. "Verily, I say unto you, Wheresoever this gospel shall be preached throughout the whole world, this also that she hath done shall be spoken of for a memorial of her." How thrilling! "Hand in hand with myself," said Jesus to Mary, "you will walk across the centuries. Wherever my story is told yours will be told also." So it has been, so it is still. As we listen to the gospel at this hour we hear once more the beautiful story of Mary.

I

Look at the picture. The scene is a dinner party in the village of Bethany. Jesus and Lazarus are the guests of honor. So far as we know the Master never refused an invitation to dinner. In spite of the fact that he knew that some of those invitations were given from mixed motives and some from positive hostility, he always accepted. But here is one that was given out of sheer friendliness. For once he is invited because he is desired and loved. This invitation he accepts in spite of the fact that his cross is only a week away. He is so close to death that he can feel its chilling breath upon his face. Yet he hides his sorrow in his heart and goes out to dinner. This he does because he cannot bear to disappoint his friends.

His host on this occasion is Simon the leper. Who Simon is we do not know. But we do know this, that he has been a leper so long that that ghastly disease has become a part of his name. He may have been that desperate and skeptical man who flung himself at the feet of Jesus, saying, "Lord, if thou wilt, thou canst make me clean." But whoever he is, of this we may be sure: that he is not a leper any more. Sometime, somewhere, he has experienced the healing power of Jesus. In all probability, therefore, he is giving this dinner to the Master out of love and gratitude.

Not only is this host thoroughly friendly, but, with the exception of Judas, so also are the guests. Peter and John and James are there, as are loyal Thomas and Matthew. By this time the enemies of Jesus have become quite numerous. It has taken real courage on the part of Simon to give this dinner. But here the hostile are shut out and Jesus has the privilege of being shut in with his friends. Another whose presence must have added to the warmth and joy of this occasion is skillful, bustling, hard-working Martha. This is not her home, yet she is in charge and is doing the serving. Instead of sending to Jerusalem for a caterer Simon has been wise enough to secure Martha, his own good friend, and the devoted friend of Jesus. He knows that none can do the task quite so well. So here she is doing what she most loves to do and what she can do the best. She is the same as when we saw her in her own home except that she is now not hot and flustered any more. She has learned from Jesus the secret of peace.

Finally, present also on this glad occasion is Mary. But she is not here to have a part in the feast. This seems to have been a dinner for men only. Nor is she helping Martha with the serving. In the scene we studied in our preceding sermon she seems to have helped her sister for a while, then to have taken her place at the feet of Jesus. But here there is no indication that she helps in the slightest either in the preparing or the serving of the dinner. I can imagine that some of the guests, as well as Martha, feel that she is a bit in the way. It may be that this feeling is shared somewhat by Mary herself. Yet she has found it impossible to stay away. This is the case because here are those whom she loves the best.

I can see her as she looks in upon the host and his guests. She knows Simon and values him as a friend.

Her heart grows warm with joy as she sees him his old self once more. There is Lazarus, who has been so marvelously restored to her. Then there is that Guest in whose honor the feast is given and to whom all owe so much. Her heart is so flooded with grateful love that she feel she must give expression to it in some fashion. Now, love is the most inventive something in the world. It will do the big thing if it can. If it cannot, it will do the small thing in a grand way. But, whether large or small, it will do something. Mary remembers her greatest treasure, a vase of precious perfume. She hurries to her home and secures it. Then she returns to break that priceless vase and anoint the head and feet of her Lord.

II

Soon everybody knows what has happened. The whole room is filled with the exquisite perfume. What is the reaction of those present?

1. We naturally expect that everybody who has the privilege of sharing the fragrance of this beautiful deed will be smiling from sheer gladness. But such is not the case. There are far more frowns than smiles, far more criticism than praise, far more indignation than approval. There is one man especially who looks at Mary with hard and critical eyes. "Why," he hisses, "was this waste of the ointment made? It might have been sold for more than three hundred pence and the proceeds given to the poor." The man who said that

is Judas. He sees in this deed of Mary's nothing to commend. At its best, it is silly, the extravagant deed of a woman emotionally unbalanced. At its worst, it is downright wicked. "Think," said Judas to those about him—"think how many hungry people there are here and in Jerusalem that this might have fed. Think how many there are in rags that this would have clothed. Mary is a silly and heartless creature who does not care for the poor. If she cared as I do, she would never have thrown this treasure away."

When Judas thus dares to speak his mind there are others who at once nod approval. Criticism is contagious. It is as catching as measles. Let anyone start yelping upon the heels of his brother, and soon others will join in the chase. "You are right, Judas," answers his neighbor; "you have your feet on the ground. You are no fanatical dreamer. Mary has done a silly and wicked and heartless thing." And under kindred circumstances we take up the hue and cry from generation to generation. We strike out blindly against those who waste their substance by doing things that we do not quite dare to do.

Recently Mr. Channing Pollock, in telling us his varied reasons for not attending church, mentioned among the rest the wastefulness of those who build churches. "These ought," he said, "to use this money for the feeding of the hungry bodies and the hungry minds of men." Having heard that bark, dozens of echoes, I dare say, took it up, and began to yap at the heels of the Church. But of course Mr. Pollock knows quite well that those who waste money in church-building are the ones, as a rule, who waste it on the feeding of the hungry bodies of men. They are also the ones who waste it upon the building of our educational institutions. Practically all of our great universities were founded by the Church. If one were to take out of our Community Chests and out of our eleemosynary institutions the money that comes from the pockets of the builders of churches, these in many instances would have to close their doors. The truth is that any fair facing of the facts will show that the people who waste money in church-building are those who waste it in building about everything else in our civilization that is worth while. Yet Judas and some of his fellow disciples see nothing in the deed of Mary except something to be condemned.

2. But Jesus sees it through different eyes. When therefore he hears this harsh criticism, he is quick to rise to the defense of his friend. "Let her alone!" he commands. I think that word had a cutting edge to it. If Judas is indignant, Jesus is more so. The Master never showed the slightest anger when he himself was wronged. But in the presence of injustice done to others his soul had a way of leaping to its feet fire-eyed and defiant. "Let her alone! Why are you annoying her? You say that she has done a wasteful and wicked thing, but I tell you that she has done a beautiful thing. She has given of her very best. Her

deed is so beautiful that I will never forget it, and I will never allow the world to forget it."

I should like to have seen Mary when she heard that word. A moment ago her face must have been burning with embarrassment as she listened to the hot words of criticism. Maybe she began to feel that she had been silly. How their criticism made her suffer! But now she feels that no suffering is too great to be born gladly if only it is followed by such commendation. Dean Swift was greatly loved by two women, Stella and Vanessa. He broke both of their hearts. They both died near him, but away from him. He had not the heart to see them die. But one said that she would have been willing to have endured his cruelty to have had his love. Be that as it may, I am sure that Mary was glad to endure any criticism from the world in order to win such warm approval from Jesus.

III

But does she deserve such high praise? Does it not seem as if the Master is a bit extravagant? Is he not allowing his chivalry to get the better of him? Has he for once become a flatterer? No; here as always he is his candid self. When he declares, therefore, that this deed, instead of being merely silly and wasteful and wicked, is really beautiful he is speaking sober truth. Wherein is it beautiful?

1. It is beautiful in its motive. "She has done a beautiful thing to me." There is no deed that we do

out of love and loyalty to Jesus that is not beautiful. This is true regardless of how silly and of how ugly and wasteful this deed may appear to the eyes of men. Even the giving of so small a gift as a cup of water cannot possibly fail of its reward. In fact, the worth or worthlessness of any gift, so far as the giver is concerned, depends upon the motive. Nothing that we do from a motive of selfishness can be beautiful. Nothing that we do for love's sake can fail in beauty. The rarest orchids given from a sordid motive become mere weeds. A paltry weed given in love may become sweeter than the loveliest rose.

That which makes the criticism of Judas and his friends ugly is that it was born of an ugly motive. Had Judas really been honest, had love for the poor been his real motive, had he been speaking his sincere convictions, his criticism would have had beauty in it, however mistaken it might have been. But he is criticizing Mary because he wants for himself what this devoted woman is giving to Jesus. His friends are criticizing partly because they feel rebuked that they do not dare to give as Mary is giving. The vast majority of our criticism is ugly because it is selfish. We feel that in tearing another down we are building ourselves up. Mary's deed is beautiful because it was done for love's sake.

2. This deed is beautiful because of its originality. Mary does not have the skill in preparing and serving meals that belongs to her sister Martha. She cannot

give what Martha is giving. But she does not allow this fact to prevent her from giving anything at all. She resolves to serve Jesus in her own way. She dares to dress her life by her own mirror. She dares to be her own lovely and lovable self. God gives to every man his work. He does not call on you to be like anyone else in the world. He does not require at your hands the gifts of another. He only asks you to give what is your very own.

This is a commonplace truth, I know, but it is one that we are very slow to learn. Martha is big-hearted and generous, but even she is slow in learning it. She feels that because Mary is not a good cook she is practically useless. I remember a certain farmer-boy years ago who at every odd hour would lay hold on some book. His father, one of the best of men, was a farmer out of sheer love of farming. But when his boy had no love for the farm and cared only for books, he thought that boy hopeless. Dr. Thompson, an English physician, had a son named Francis. He determined that Francis should follow in his steps, that he should dedicate his life to the art of healing. But Francis had no heart for it. He rebelled, fled to London, and went to the dogs. It was only when he was privileged to make his own gift in his own way that he became one of the sweetest singers in English literature. Dare to follow your own inner voice. Dare in this wholesome and sane sense to live your own life.

3. This deed is beautiful in its abandon. Mary

might have anointed her Lord with a small fraction of her treasure, but with mad recklessness she throws it all away on one adventure. That is exactly what Jesus finds so thrillingly beautiful. He never has a word of praise for prudent and conservative giving. His delighted approval goes only to those who give with abandon. For instance, he grows enthusiastic over the two mites of the widow, not because they are so much, but because they are her all. He is thrilled by the beauty of Mary's gift because it is her very best. To her he gives the finest word of praise that is possible. "She hath done what she could." To do one's best is the very highest possible achievement.

But here is a startling word. Though the finest possible for any of us is to do our best, that is also the least we can do and be truly Christian. It is not a question of how much we give or of how much we achieve. It is a question of the fullness of the dedication of our gifts. Some who have accomplished little will meet the divine approval, while others who have accomplished far more will be condemned. It is only to those who have given their best that Jesus will be able to say, "Well done." The beauty of Mary's gift is beautiful, therefore, because it is her whole-hearted best.

4. Her deed is beautiful in its helpfulness. I am not forgetting that Judas has just said that it did no good at all. He has just declared that the whole treasure was wasted, that it went for nothing. But we need

to remember that Judas has no scales for the weighing of life's finest values. He thinks anything worthless that one cannot deposit in the bank or serve on a dish. He does not know that the most priceless things often seem to be worthless. How trifling, for instance, is a smile! Yet under certain circumstances a smile may be more valuable than diamonds. There are times when a kiss may be more healing than medicine. There come situations when a bit of appreciation may prove of more value than countless treasure.

We may be sure that this deed of Mary's helps Jesus far more than all else that was done for him that day. He appreciates the friendship of Simon, he deeply appreciates Martha's serving, but Mary's anointing proves far more helpful than all these. Her gift is born of an insight deeper than that of any other of his friends. Mary has an understanding heart. She knows as none other what Jesus is suffering. Her loving eyes see deeper into his heartache than those of any other. Jesus declares that her gift is to prepare his body for the burial. Not only so, but it is already helping prepare him for the hard ordeal of the cross. No other person, I think, understands Jesus as does Mary. Because of this, her gift was helpful above that of all others.

Not only does Mary help Jesus by this gift as none other helped, but she also helps the poor as she could have helped in no other way. Suppose she had followed the sane advice of Judas and had sold her gift and had given the proceeds to the poor; that would have been beautiful. But had she done so her deed would in all probability have been forgotten centuries ago. But by giving it as she did, she has helped rich and poor alike for nineteen hundred years. At this hour the sweet perfume that filled Simon's house in the long ago envelops us. All of us, I trust, are a bit better because of Mary's lovely deed. How often it is true that the most practical use we can make both of our gifts and of ourselves is to use them in a fashion that seems to the critical eyes of Judas most impractical and foolish. Mary's gift is beautiful in its helpfulness.

5. Finally, Mary's deed is beautiful in its timing. Many a deed that might have been beautiful has attained only ugliness because it was not timed aright. Some time ago a young chap who had broken his mother's heart came home to see that mother die. As he bent above her still face, he spilled out hot words of confession and love along with his tears. But the mother did not change her expression by so much as the moving of an eyelash. His coming thus would have helped her beyond words had it been right in its timing.

But he came too late. She had passed beyond the hearing of his voice. At a funeral the other day there was a floral offering for a wife that was amazingly beautiful. The only tragedy was in its timing. If her husband had brought her the smallest field flower six months before, it would have been worth more to her than all the flowers that ever bloomed were worth as she lay asleep.

Listen to what Jesus says of this beautiful deed: "She is come aforehand to anoint my body to the burying." Nicodemus loved Jesus. After he was dead he brought him a wealth of precious spices and perfume. But his timing was bad. But Mary, with the fine intuition of love, looks down the road and sees death coming toward her Master. "I will beat death to him," she vows; "I will anoint him before death arrives." And so she does. And when death comes and touches him, a bit later, her gift makes even his frozen fingers smell of perfume. Many of our otherwise lovely deeds lose their value because of bad timing. Therefore, if you have a good word to say to your friend, say it now. If you have any helpful gift to make, make it now.

" 'Tis easy to be gentle when death's silence stills our
  clamor,
 'Tis easy to discern the best through memorie's mys-
   tic glamor,
   But O 'twere well for me and thee, ere love is past
    forgiving,
   To take this simple lesson home, be patient with the
    living."

Now, one of the glories of this story is that it puts this high commendation of Jesus within reach of every one of us. We have our varied gifts, temperaments, and talents. I cannot do what you can do, and you cannot do what I can do. But we can all act from motives of love. We can all give what is in our hands and hearts. We can all do our best. To do that is to do the most practical and helpful thing in the world. To do that is to help enrich both ourselves and others for time and for eternity. How much of your treasure, how much of your life, how much of your self do you propose to keep? All that you keep you will lose. All that you give away you will keep. This is plain common sense. God grant that we may so act that our Lord may say of us, "He has done a beautiful thing to me."

XV

THE EXPECTANT FACE

"She came up just at that time .... and spoke about the child to all who were living in expectation of the liberation."

LUKE 2:38 (GOODSPEED)

THIS PROPHETESS, ANNA, HAD A WORD FOR THE expectant. She was able to speak their language because she shared, even in a greater richness than themselves, their high hopes. Her lot was cast in a difficult day. Life for the vast majority had become dull and drab and gray. But in spite of her environment, in spite of the fact that she was now very old, in spite of the further fact that she had known bereavement, loneliness, and tears, her face was still strangely radiant. In truth, it seemed to be illuminated by an inner light. In spite of the marks and scars that time and tears had made, it was still so transfigured as to remind us of "an old crumbling village church lighted for service." The secret of this radiance is the fact that Anna was living in expectation.

I

This being the case, I think we might do well to sit at the feet of this woman of the long ago. Her secret is worth learning because expectation is a prize to be coveted. "Of course," you answer readily. But it is not "of course" at all. There are multitudes that are afraid of any high expectation. We have a beatitude that is just about as well known and as heartily believed as any that was uttered by our Master. It runs like this: "Blessed are they that expect nothing, for they shall not be disappointed." We must recognize that there is some bit of truth in this beatitude. That is the reason it has lived. A lie that is a hundred per cent lie soon dies. That which is true about this beatitude is that the expectant are often disappointed. However fortunate and successful we may be, all our dreams never come true. Every one of us knows the pain of disappointed hopes.

Because this is true there are those who have become afraid to hope. Did not one of the most brilliant women in America say recently that she would never dare to love again? She had been so bitterly disappointed in her other loves that she was afraid to love any more. Some time ago I was out during a dark night of storm. Suddenly there was a lurid flash of lightning that illuminated the landscape for an instant. But the darkness that followed made the night seem blacker than before. So some of our high expectations have lighted our path for a moment and have left us in deeper darkness. That is what Lord Morley meant when he said, "For the wettest of wet blankets give me the man who was most enthusiastic in his youth."

Some years ago while visiting in a certain home I met a woman whose face was little more than a blank mask of despair. I learned something of her history. In the sweet radiance of her girlhood she had had a love affair. She had staked everything on that glad adventure. By and by she was to be married. The date was set, the guests were gathered, the minister had come, the wedding cake was upon the table, she was dressed in her bridal attire. But the bridegroom never came. She felt herself not only cheated of her hope, but shamed and disgraced. From that disappointing experience she went to throw herself away. Her whole after-life was in a sense a proclamation of the blessedness of those who expect nothing.

You remember how Andrew Carnegie built a fortune. But his chief interest was not in money. He helped scores of cities to build splendid libraries. But the biggest passion of his life, at least during his later years, was world peace. With a passion akin to that of the prophets, he looked forward to that good day when men should learn war no more. In fact, he came to believe that that day had already come. He hailed it with joy. But even while he was thrilling with this high hope, the first World War broke out. He watched one nation after another slip into that abysm of blood and tears until almost the whole world was involved. The disappointment was too bitter for him. He died in large measure of a broken heart.

But if expectation is dangerous, the lack of it is more dangerous still. If I go to bat with high expectation, I may be disappointed when I strike out. But if I never expect to make a hit, I will not dare go to bat at all. Therefore, in spite of the risks, I am going on expecting. I am going to keep looking for Santa Claus. If he fails to come, of course my stocking will be empty. But, even then, it will not be more empty than that of the man who did not look for him. Besides, I shall have had at least the fun of expecting him. Any disappointment is better than never to have hoped.

> "I envy not in any moods
>   The captive void of noble rage,
>   The linnet born within the cage
> That never knew the summer woods : . . . .
>
> "Nor, what may count itself as blest,
>   The heart that never plighted troth,
>   But stagnates in the weeds of sloth ;
> Nor any want-begotten rest.
>
> "I hold it true whate'er befall ;
>   I feel it when I sorrow most ;
>   'Tis better to have loved and lost
> Than never to have loved at all." [1]

[1] Alfred Tennyson, "In Memoriam," xxvii.

II

But if expectation is a prize to be desired, what is the good of it?

1. Expectation gives a tang to the feast of life. It brings a thrill to the dawning of every new day. Without it life loses its song. So important is expectation that if we miss it, though we might gain all other prizes, life for us would still be dull and gray. So important is it that if it continues to be our possession, though, if it were possible, we might miss all else, life would still be vastly interesting and vastly worth while. If we have expectation as our companion every desert becomes a bit of garden. If we miss it, even the choicest of gardens becomes a desert.

Take the cynic in Ecclesiastes, for instance. He had about everything. He had vast wealth. He had position and power. He had a keen and discerning mind. But lacking expectancy he lived under leaden skies, and there was no thrill of immortal music in his heart. He was keen enough to discern the wickedness growing out of man's inhumanity to man. But he was not gripped by the passion of the crusader. He saw no hope of making things better. He was sure that the crooked could never be made straight. Things were bad yesterday, they were going to continue to be bad today and tomorrow. "What has been will be," he declared, "and there is no new thing under the sun." Living thus without expectation life was as ashes upon his lips. He summed up its significance in these bitter words, "Vanity of vanities, all is vanity and vexation of spirit."

But here is another man, Paul by name. He has missed much that the cynic has won. In the days of his youth he had been ambitious for leadership in his church. But by and by Christ took captive his heart. In his loyalty to his new-found Lord he tells us that he suffered the loss of all things. Again and again he knew the shame and pain of the whipping post. He perhaps knew the inside of more jails than any other man in the Roman Empire. He is in jail now with few friends and without clothing enough to keep him warm. He writes to devoted Timothy to come and bring his coat, and to do so if possible before winter. But though he has suffered the loss of all things he has a light in his face brighter than the light of stars. It is the light of a great expectation. "Henceforth," he sings, "there is laid up for me a crown of righteousness, which the Lord, the righteous judge, shall give me at that day." If we have lost hope, all treasure is so much fairy gold. If we are rich in expectancy, we can get on without almost all else.

2. Expectation is a pathway of discovery. It is expectation that gives us eyes to see. This is the case in what we call the physical. Who have discovered and mapped this world upon which we live? This has been the achievement of the expectant. Naturally some of these explorers have found more than they expected. But those who have been satisfied with the little

strip of land upon which they lived, those who have refused to believe that there was anything beyond, have never been the discoverers. "They that go down to the sea in ships, that do business in great waters; these see the works of the Lord, and his wonders in the deep." These see because they are expectant enough to venture. As the expectant have discovered all the continents, so also have they made all the scientific discoveries. Every great scientist has lived on tiptoe of expectancy. Those who have expected nothing have seen nothing.

Just as the expectant are the discoverers in the realm of the physical, so also are they the discoverers in the realm of the spiritual. Who recognized the Christ in that little child born in the manger of Bethlehem? Only a few shepherds, saintly Simeon, this woman Anna. Why did they recognize him? It was not because he wore a halo about his baby brow; he did not. They recognized him because they were looking for him. There was a prophet in the long ago who declared that he would set him upon his watchtower, that he would keep his face turned toward the eastern horizon in anticipation of the rising of the Son of Righteousness. Because he was thus expectant, God was able to reveal himself to him. The expectant are forever finding fountains where those without expectation see only the hot sands of the desert.

3. Then, expectation is a mark of unfailing youth. One of the choicest characteristics of youth is its hopefulness. Every youthful Alice lives in Wonderland.

The world of childhood and youth is not only full of undiscovered wonders, but it is full of high possibilities. However wrong that world may be, there is a possibility of setting it right. However dark it may be, there is ever the hope of the breaking of a new day. So long as this expectancy is ours we can never grow old. Now and then some benighted church official will say, "We need a young pastor to appeal to our young people." That is true, but how many birthdays the pastor has had has nothing to do with his appeal. Youth is a matter of the heart. If you still believe that the impossible can become possible, then you are young whether you are eighteen or eighty. If you have lost this expectation you are old, however few your birthdays.

4. Finally, expectation is a source of usefulness. The expectant man is useful by virtue of what he is. Look at this scene on board an ancient merchantship. For many days now that ship has been the plaything of a tempest. Soldiers and sailors have done their best to make the vessel secure, but in spite of all their efforts it is going to pieces. Death is laughing with hollow laughter among the torn shreds of the rigging. "All hope that we should be saved," says an eyewitness, "was then taken away." But that lost hope came back, the men rallied and were saved to a man. How did it come about? It came about through the hopefulness of one Paul who stood up in the face of the storm to say,

"I believe God." The expectant man helps by being expectant.

Then, expectation is a source of usefulness because it leads to action. What, for instance, is the radio doing for about twenty-five hours out of twenty-four? It is proclaiming all sorts of wares. It tells us of the cigarettes that satisfy, it tells us of how we may be cured of every kind of disease. It is seeking to excite expectation in the realization that expectation brings about action. It is said that on the eve of a hog-callers' contest in Kansas, the coach was instructing the contestants as to the qualifications of a winner. "To call hogs effectively," he said, "two qualifications are necessary. First, the caller must have enough volume to make the hogs hear him. Second, he must have enough appeal in his voice to make the hogs think that he has something they want." There you have it! Expectation leads to action.

Here is one secret of the irresistible might of the early Church. This Church won its triumphs in one of the darkest and most desperate days of human history. How were these saints able to go from victory to victory? One source of their power was their expectation. They had a word with which they constantly cheered each other on. That word was "Maranatha" (the Lord is coming). They lived in daily expectation of the visible return of Jesus Christ. They were sure that any day, any hour, any moment the heavens might blaze with his glory and that he might come to set up his Kingdom in the earth. Nerved by this hope they were unconquered and unconquerable. They drew to themselves countless thousands of unexpectant souls who were eager to share their radiant hopes.

Sad to say, we who compose the Church of today have largely lost that bracing expectancy. We realize that the early saints were mistaken in looking for a visible coming of their Lord. But the fact that they were mistaken about the method of his coming does not mean that they were wrong in expecting him at all. We believe that his coming is continuous. Any hour, any moment he is ready to reveal himself to those who have eyes to see. But our tragedy is that most of us have ceased to expect him. That is the reason that our services are so often listless and dull. But today where worshipers come together in the assurance of meeting the risen Christ, there the atmosphere is tense with a joyous expectancy that can be found nowhere else. It is the expectant church that has drawing power. It is the expectant church that is the hope of the world.

III

How then are we to be expectant? How are we to keep this prize if it is ours? How are we to achieve it if we have lost it?

Let us realize at once that this expectation is not a mere matter of temperament. There are some who dismiss the whole subject by saying, "Well, some folks are naturally hopeful while others are naturally pessimistic." But this expectancy that transfigured the face of Anna is not a mere matter of temperament. I know there are some who are more hopeful than others. There are some who seem to live their lives in the sunshine, while others cling about the shadows as ivy about old ruins. But this rare blossom that grew in the garden of Anna's heart requires a far more fertile soil than mere temperament. Those who are naturally optimistic often lose their optimism. Then those who are naturally pessimistic may come to possess faces transfigured by expectation.

What, then, I repeat, is the secret of this expectation? Anna had learned it through long fellowship with God. That is the way for ourselves. Here is a prayer from the lips of a man who lived expectantly in the face of opposition that was enough to break the stoutest heart. Listen! "The God of hope fill you with all joy and peace in believing, that ye may abound in hope, through the power of the Holy Ghost." The first fact that this tells us is that our God is a hopeful God. Isaiah made that discovery and declared. "He shall not fail nor be discouraged." What a tremendous assertion that is! Think of the tragedies upon which God has had to look through the centuries. Think of the tragedies upon which he looks today. Yet from eternity to eternity our God is a God of hope.

Since our God is a God of hope he inspires hope in those who know him. We can gather hope as we turn our eyes to the wonders that he has wrought in yesterday. Think of how near he came to you in the darkest experience that ever came into your life. Think of how, when all seemed lost, you found his grace sufficient. In fact, he has done far more for you than merely to enable you to bear your sorrow. In ways past belief he has changed your sorrow into joy, your want into wealth. As you think on what he did yesterday and on what he is doing today, you find hope for tomorrow. "He rescued me," shouts Paul, looking back upon a trying experience. "He rescued me, he rescues still, and I rely on him for the hope that he will continue to rescue me."

Not only can we gather hope as we look at God's dealing with our own lives, but we can do so as we watch him deal with the great tragedies of human history. No greater blow was ever struck at goodness than was struck on Calvary. Yet that cross has become the supreme magnet of mankind. Then we think of the despots that today threaten to wreck the world. The outlook has never before seemed to us so black. But such tragedies are not new to God. In far-off yesterdays other nations have crushed their fellows. But their victories were temporary. Every one of them is now among the dead. From this I think that we may take hope that the final victory in our day is not going to be with the forces of evil, but with the forces of righteousness.

I am indebted to another for this story. A seasoned

mountain-climber set out in company with a young novice to conquer one of the peaks of the Pyrenees. Before they reached their goal night came on and they were obliged to camp on the shelf of a cliff. They were awakened by a fierce storm. Lurid lightnings leaped from crag to crag, and the thunders crashed with such horror that the young fellow was filled with fear. At last he turned to his companion with the declaration, "The world is coming to an end!" But the seasoned climber answered quietly, "Don't be afraid; that is the way the dawn comes in the Pyrenees. This storm does not mean the end of the world; it means only the dawning of a new day." Let us dare to expect that to be the outcome of the storm that now shakes our world. Surely that will be the outcome of the storm in our individual lives if we keep expectantly within the will of God.

XVI

THE WISTFUL FACE

"If thou knewest the gift of God, and who it is that saith to thee, Give me to drink; thou wouldest have asked of him, and he would have given thee living water."

JOHN 4:10

IT IS NOONDAY. JESUS, WHO HAS BEEN TRAVELING on foot, is resting a bit. He has chosen as his place of rest an old well-curb. At present he is alone. His friends have gone into the village of Sychar to buy food for the noonday meal. As Jesus looks across the plain toward this village he sees a woman coming with her water-pitcher upon her shoulder. It is rather unusual that she should come for water in the heat of the day. The reason that she is doing so is because she dreads the hot rays of the sun less than she dreads the hot scorn and contempt of her respectable sisters.

I

There are three facts about this woman to which I wish to call your attention.

1. The first is a matter of common knowledge. Everybody knows it who knows her at all. She is an outcast woman. Years ago, perhaps when quite young, she had married. Maybe she had entered into this beautiful relationship with high hopes and fine dreams. Maybe she had been cheap and flippant from the beginning. Maybe she had dragged her orange-blossoms through the mud by running away with another man. Then she might have been more sinned against than sinning. Her husband might have been a bit of a brute who made a hell of their humble home. Be that as it may, her first marriage had gone upon the rocks. But since hope springs eternal in the human breast she had made a second venture. But this also ended in disaster. Then had followed a third, then a fourth, then a fifth. In fact, marriage became a habit. She had flitted from one husband to another as a bird flits from branch to branch in a tree. Thus, it is evident that she was a very modern woman. She would have felt very much at home in our city or in Hollywood.

But having made five failures she has at last given up the struggle. "Why go through the formality of a ceremony any more?" she asked herself. "Why promise to cleave unto a man till death when I know that my marriage will last only till the first sharp quarrel, or till we grow weary of each other?" So she decided that a further marriage would be useless. From now on she would take her man where she found him and live with him as long as it suited her. She must have had some charm. Perhaps she had once been beautiful. Certainly she was quite intelligent. Her conversation indicates that she was a woman of sharp wit. But she had given up all claim to respectability and was now living with a man who was not her husband. This fact was no dark secret. Everybody who knew her was aware of what she was.

2. Then there was a second fact about this woman, I dare say, that was known only to Jesus and to herself. Everybody knew that she not only had an evil past, but a soiled and sordid present. But there was one fact about her that her friends did not know. There was one fact that was not known even to the man with whom she was then living. It was known only to this Man on the well-curb and to herself. The fact was this: she was terribly dissatisfied with life as she was living it. However hard she tried to shut her eyes, however desperately she dissipated, there were times when she looked at herself with almost infinite disgust. There were times when she hated herself for what she was.

Naturally she had never dreamed of making the mess of her life that she had made. If ten years ago a friend had had the wisdom to point to her present self and say, "You will be like that one day," she would not have believed it. She would have been filled at once with indignation and horror. But, taking one wrong step after another, she had become what she now was.

She had journeyed to the depths in which she now found herself. She tried to brazen it out, tried to act as if she did not care. With almost everybody she got away with it. They felt that she was not only an outcast, but that she was content to be an outcast. But she could not get away with it with herself. She was desperately sick of what she had become. She knew it and Jesus knew it.

Being sick of what she was, she genuinely longed to be different. At times the gnawing hunger at her heart made her wretched. At times her burning thirst would not let her sleep. Even while she went down she often looked wistfully toward the heights and longed to climb. Once she had tried to pray. But that was in a more hopeful yesterday. By now she had given up prayer. This she had done, not because she had become satisfied to be what she was. She had given it up because she had lost hope of ever being better. The only reason that she did not then and there make of that well-curb an altar of prayer was because she did not think it would do any good. That is what Jesus was telling her when he said, "If thou knewest the gift of God, ... thou wouldest have asked of him."

The wistfulness of this woman is a characteristic of our race. It belongs to the very worst of mankind. Jesus told the story of a young chap who became gripped by the conviction that life at home was a rather mean and starved affair. He convinced himself that if he could only get into the big world beyond the hills where he could be independent of his father, then he would find life rich and full. So one day he asked for his wealth and turned his back on the restraints of home to have his fling in a far country. He lived lavishly. To all appearances at first he was having a great time. Some doubtless envied him. How fine to be a play-boy like that! But one day he faced the facts about himself. He told just how good a time he was having. He expressed it in these words, "I perish with hunger."

But this wistfulness is not a characteristic only of the great moral failures; it is even more so of the choicest of men. What an honored and religious man was Nicodemus! He had given the best years of his life to the service of the church. He had tried hard to do his duty. He had tithed faithfully and taught earnestly. But now, after all these years of willing service, he was strangely restless and wistful. So much was this the case that one night he defied his fears in order to visit a certain young Carpenter who had made himself an object of hate to all the higher-ups of Jerusalem. "He has a secret that I do not possess, a satisfaction for which I so deeply long," this master in Israel told himself as he crept through the dark. The wistfulness, then, of this outcast woman belongs to all of us, to the best as well as to the worst.

3. The third fact about this woman was known to Jesus alone. Jesus knew along with others that she was an outcast. He knew along with the woman that she

was not content to be an outcast. He alone knew that she did not have to continue to be an outcast. Everybody else had given her up. She had given herself up. She had lost heart and hope. Had you said to her as she set out for the well: "Rachel, this is going to be a momentous experience for you. You have gone to the well many times before and have returned just as you went. But such is not going to be the case this time. Though as you go you walk as through the fetid filth of a moral swamp, when you return your feet will be turned toward the lily lands of purity"—had you spoken to her in this fashion, she would probably have been indignant. "I know and you know," she might have answered, "that I can never be different. I have tried, God knows I have. But it is impossible. Decent folks refuse to give me a chance. Therefore I must run with the wolves or starve."

But Jesus reversed the verdict of the crowd and the verdict of the woman herself to declare that she could be different. Of all the characteristics of Jesus, none is more thrilling than this confidence in even the most hopeless of men and women. He believed that every man had in him a capacity for Christlikeness. Luther Burbank used to say, "Every weed is a possible flower." That is an amazing word. What a marvelous confidence he had in weeds. He was sure that the only reason the sour dock is not a plant of sweetness and light was that nobody had taken the time and pains to bring it to its possibilities. He was sure that the only reason the burweed did not have its hands full of blossoms instead of cockleburs was that nobody cared for its soul. In like manner Jesus saw in every coward a possible hero, in every sinner a possible saint. Therefore he said, "If thou knewest the gift of God, and who it is that saith to thee, Give me to drink; thou wouldest have asked of him, and he would have given thee living water." He pledged himself then and there to make the impossible possible in her life.

II

But how is this woman of the wistful face to find that treasure for which she longs even though her longing is without hope?

1. Jesus indicates that the first step is for her to realize who it is that is talking to her. Who is it that is disturbing her now? Who is it that is bringing to a climax her utter dissatisfaction with what she is? The one who is doing that is Jesus himself. He is a man, but he is more. He is one who can say, "He that hath seen me hath seen the Father." It is God in Christ who is stirring and wooing here. He is always the prime mover in our salvation. The fact that you are heart-hungry, the fact that you are yearning to be better than you are, is an indication that the God for whom you long is even now with you. Your very wistfulness is an indication that the Good Shepherd is even now seeking and finding the sheep that was lost.

2. The second fact that this woman needs to realize

in order to be different is that salvation is a gift. "If thou knewest the gift of God," said Jesus. There is that in our proud human nature that makes us eager to win salvation through merit. We desire, as did Simon Magus of old, in some fashion to buy it. But this is impossible. The salvation that Jesus offers is nothing other than himself. "The gift of God is eternal life through Jesus Christ our Lord." Since God comes to us as a gift we do not have to drag him into our hearts by force. We do not have to climb up to him; we only have to receive him. The key word of the gospel is this, "receive ye." Since this is the case, newness of life is within reach of all of us, the decent Elder Brother and the Prodigal, the respectable and the outcast, ordinary failures like ourselves and the more tragic failures such as this woman.

3. Finally, this woman needs to know that since salvation is a gift the one condition of our receiving it is that we ask. "If thou knewest the gift of God, and who it is that saith to thee, Give me to drink; thou wouldest have asked of him, and he would have given thee living water." What is Jesus saying? Just this: "You are not yet remade. You have not yet received the living water. But the one reason for your failure is not my unwillingness or inability to give, but your refusal to ask. Already you might have been enjoying newness of life if you had only dared ask for it. Even yet it may be yours if you will only claim it." "Ask,

and it shall be given you," is the promise of Jesus to this outcast, and to all of us.

But here we meet vigorous and honest objections. "I have asked," a man said recently, "but nothing came of it. I used to pray and pray earnestly, but I quit because I found that it was sheer futility." Naturally there is a kind of asking that brings no beneficial results. The asking that is effective must be the kind that is willing to co-operate with God. It is futile to ask God to show us a sunrise if we keep our faces toward the west. It is useless for a farmer to ask God for a good harvest if he refuses to plow the ground and sow the seed. It is equally useless to ask God for newness of life if we insist on continuing in the old life.

So this woman found. "Sir, give me this water," she prayed. But Jesus did not immediately grant her request. He did not because he could not. There was something in the way. She must be willing to face and forsake her sin. Therefore he said, "Go, call thy husband, and come hither." "I have no husband," came the honest answer. "Right," said Jesus. "You have had five husbands and the man whom you now have is not your husband. In that you have told the truth."

Thus the woman has been made to face her guilt. But with marvelous tact Jesus puts his emphasis, not on what is bad in her, but upon what is good. He compliments her because she has told him the truth. He expresses his appreciation for that one little white flower that is yet growing in the neglected garden of her soul. The woman cannot help but feel kindly toward him in spite of the fact that he has made her see herself. But she is quite uncomfortable. She feels that she must justify herself in some fashion. Therefore she hastens to affirm that her problem is not moral, but intellectual. She has not lived as she has because she is weak and wicked, but because she is confused. She cannot decide where she ought to worship, here at Gerizim, or yonder at Jerusalem.

How old that is, and yet how new! That has been said countless thousands of times. Here, for instance, is a man who in a time of desperate need is counting for nothing. If he is not wasting his substance in riotous living he is wasting it in respectable and selfish living. Why does he not carry his part of the load? He has a ready answer. "I would throw in my lot with those who are trying to help, but there are so many churches, and I have never been able to decide which church is right." But the real reason that this man does nothing is not because he does not know enough, but it is because he is not willing to live up to what he does know. "You may worship anywhere," Jesus said to this woman, "if you are willing to pay the price of worship. That price is complete self-dedication."

Routed from this position she now retreats to her last line of defense. She will ask sometime, but not now. "You say that I may worship God anywhere?" she seems to say. "Perhaps you are right. Still there are many things that I do not understand. Really, since I have no head for matters of religion, the whole business seems a bit up in the air. But the Messiah is coming soon; he will tell me what I ought to know. Therefore I am not going to ask for this living water today, I am going to wait for some tomorrow." "You do not have to wait," Jesus answers. "The Messiah is here now. I that speak unto thee am he. The only place that you can ask is here, the only time is now." Thus driven from all her hiding places the woman brought her request into the living present.

III

What was the result?

Having brought her asking into the present tense, she begins then and there to receive. Then and there she begins to walk in newness of life. In the joy of her amazing discovery she forgets her errand. She is no longer interested in the water of Jacob's well. Therefore she leaves her pitcher to hurry back toward Sychar. "Where are you going?" I ask, not knowing what has taken place in her life. "I am going to share with others what I have found for myself. I am going to tell them about Jesus."

How absurd! I am ready to break into loud and cynical laughter. "You are going to tell about Jesus?" I answer. "Don't be silly. Who will listen to you? Who will believe you? Why, the very street-boys know you. Everybody knows that you have been blown like a filthy rag about the streets of this city for years."

THE WISTFUL FACE

But she is too joyous and too eager to listen to me. In spite of her sordid past she keeps on her way. With what result? We find the answer in these words: "Many .... believed on him because of the word of the woman." Somehow, when even the most unpromising become sure of God, they have that to share for which all the world dimly longs.

This human story comes very close to our day. We do not make as much of the matter of sin, perhaps, as did our fathers. We do not talk of salvation in the same terms as they. But there is something that we share with them and with this outcast woman—we are all wistful and heart-hungry. Even many of us who have been in the church for years feel that our religion has been little better than a disappointment. Though we have a form of godliness, the power, the winsome reality, is strangely lacking. To your heart and mine, therefore, I bring this ever-new invitation. It is as fresh today as when it was first given: "Ho, every one that thirsteth, come ye to the waters." "If any man thirst, let him come unto me, and drink. He that believeth on me, as the scripture hath said, out of his inner life shall flow rivers of living water." If you want something to satisfy and something to share, you will find it as you accept this invitation, and you will find it nowhere else.